GARDENWALKS

IN THE MID-ATLANTIC STATES

Beautiful Gardens from
New York to Washington, D.C.

MARINA HARRISON *and* LUCY D. ROSENFELD

INSIDERS' GUIDE®

GUILFORD, CONNECTICUT
AN IMPRINT OF THE GLOBE PEQUOT PRESS

Garden admission fees and hours are subject to change. We recommend that you contact establishments before traveling to obtain current information.

INSIDERS' GUIDE®

Text design by Diane Gleba Hall
Illustrations by Ted Enik
Maps created by Ted Enik © The Globe Pequot Press

Library of Congress Cataloging-in-Publication Data

Harrison, Marina, 1939–
    Gardenwalks in the mid-Atlantic states/Marina Harrison and Lucy D. Rosenfeld—1st ed.
        p. cm.—(Gardenwalks series)
    ISBN 0-7627-3669-0
        1. Gardens—Middle Atlantic States—Guidebooks. 2. Middle Atlantic States—Guidebooks. I. Rosenfeld, Lucy D., 1939– II. Title. III. Series.

    SB466.U65M524 2005
    712'.0974—dc22

                                            2005041925

Manufactured in the United States of America
First Edition/First Printing

Contents

v   Preface

1   Thoughts on Garden Styles

33   Gardenwalks in Delaware

43   Gardenwalks in Maryland

59   Gardenwalks in New Jersey

91   Gardenwalks in New York

    92   *New York City*

    121   *Hudson Valley*

    154   *Long Island*

    169   *Upstate New York*

181 Gardenwalks in Pennsylvania

217 Choosing an Outing

224 Garden Shows and Festivals

226 Glossary

229 Index of Gardens

Preface

$\mathcal{T}$HIS BOOK invites garden lovers to join us in a search for beautiful and interesting sights. While we don't pretend to be horticulturalists, botanists, or even to have very green thumbs ourselves, we do know an aesthetic treat when we see one!

As you may know from our previous guidebooks, we are inveterate walkers and connoisseurs of exceptional art and scenery. The gardens we have selected in the Mid-Atlantic region provide both natural and aesthetic pleasures. We describe in some detail our favorite gardens, which reflect the melting-pot aspects of our nation, ranging in style from the most eccentric personal expressions to the traditional formal elegance of European and Asian origins. We have not overlooked natural and wildflower preserves, which some people consider the best gardens of all. Also included are sculpture and architectural gardens; conservatories and indoor gardens; specialty gardens, such as an all-peony garden; gardens for the disabled; Asian gardens; gardens with great views, whose very settings make them special; and some intriguing private gardens, whose owners have graciously invited visitors. You'll find at the end of each state chapter a heading called "Don't Miss . . .," which features write-ups of other worthy garden sites.

We have tried to introduce our readers to various historic, multinational, and artistic garden designs in a chapter at the beginning of the book called "Thoughts on Garden Styles." Near the end of the book is "Choosing an Outing," a guide that will help you select a garden to visit by style or tradition.

Every garden in this book is open to the public on a more or less regular basis in season; we have not included gardens open only one day a year. While we cannot—in a useful, portable guide—fully describe every choice garden in the Mid-Atlantic, we have given a thumbnail sketch of those you should not miss as you travel around the region.

We include many unexpected treats in this book in addition to many well-known, well-loved sites. For instance, you may be surprised to find several delightful gardens nestled among the bustling streetscapes of New York City. Of course the city offers the glamorous Brooklyn Botanical Garden, the inimitable New York Botanical Garden in the Bronx, and the city's crowning jewel, its great Central Park, a landscape designed by Frederick Law Olmsted. But we also refer you to delightful, smallish oases in the heart of the city. They are places to rest and contemplate startling aesthetic beauty just around the corner or across the street from the urban cacophony we know as New York. You may wish to spend a lunch hour, or a respite after work, or a weekend afternoon exploring several small, special gardens.

We have spent several years visiting every sort of garden in every season—on beautiful sunny days as well as in pouring rain. Wherever we have gone, we have been given enthusiastic and helpful suggestions. Many people have directed us to gardens we might have overlooked, and others have recommended books and garden tours and have even led us to hard-to-find places themselves. This collection of gardens is one of several we have written. You'll enjoy our *Gardenwalks in New England* and our forthcoming book about gardenwalks in the South.

Gardens are by definition fragile. As living environments they are subject to the whims and changes of nature—and nurture. As we wrote this book, all the gardens we describe were in good condition and welcomed visitors. We hope you will find them as pleasing and carefully tended as we have.

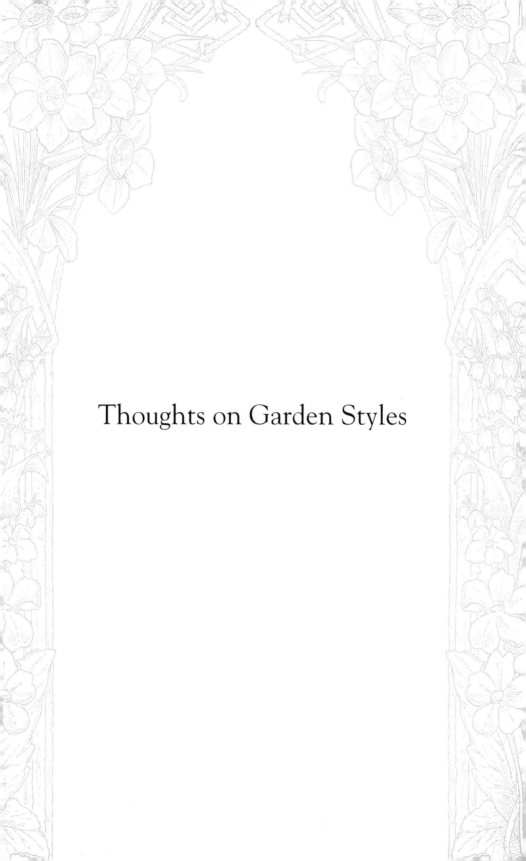

Thoughts on Garden Styles

Formal and Informal Gardens

> "Romanticism" is an idea which needed a Classical mind
> to have it.
>
> —J. F. SHADE (1898–1959)

AMONG THE fundamental questions that have defined land-scape design in America and other Western countries is the issue of formal versus naturalistic gardens. Should a garden focus on structure and architecture or on its plantings? Should it be arranged in geometric patterns, or in a flowing, more random manner reflecting a natural landscape?

The formal approach has its cultural roots in the traditions of Italy and France. Formal gardens in the Italian and French style share important similarities. Both are regarded as architectural extensions of the house; both emphasize structure, symmetry, and classical motifs, such as statues and balustraded terraces; and in both, plants are considered subordinate to the overall design.

The first Italian gardens (as we know them today) appeared during the Renaissance, especially in the regions surrounding Florence and Rome, where some of the most important patrons, sculptors, and architects lived and worked. Villas were built as rural retreats from the city, much like their predecessors in antiquity. Their gardens, linking the house to the surrounding countryside, were designed to be ideal sites for contemplating and experiencing nature. At carefully chosen sites, viewers were invited to enjoy sweeping vistas of the formal layout and the countryside beyond.

The ideal Italian Renaissance garden—elegant, proportioned, and symmetrical—represented a harmonious balance between nature and architecture. Here nature was tamed and ordered into neatly clipped evergreens of laurel, box, and yew shaped into elaborate mazes and borders. Stone and marble forms—colonnaded stairways, terraces, and statues depicting allegorical and mythological characters—were essential elements of this style. So too was water. The Villa d'Este at Tivoli, with its spectacular fountains, cascades, and basins—and amazing waterpowered mechanisms—is one of the most magnificent Renaissance gardens of all.

The Medici family of Florence helped introduce Italian garden designs to France, as did migrating Italian artisans and gardeners. The formal gardens of seventeenth-century France represented a new interpretation of these ideals. To a substantially greater degree than Italian gardens, these totally controlled landscapes symbolized humanity's mastery of the natural world.

Essential to French formal gardens were ornamental garden beds (parterres) fashioned from exquisitely shaped boxwood and yew. These intricate geometric compartments with squares, circles, and ovals were flawless in their symmetrical designs. They could be viewed from the formal reception rooms of the house overlooking them, or along an orderly grid of walkways. Sometimes complementing them were rows of small trees or shrubs shaped into topiary forms. (Topiaries in Italy tended to represent whimsical creatures, while those in France were strictly geometric and abstract.)

Versailles, the great masterpiece of André Le Nôtre, is certainly the most noted garden in the French style. Everything in it was laid out to symbolize the triumph of humanity (more specifically, the Sun King) over nature, from its majestic proportions and perspectives, to the central axis leading to broad vistas, to the grand canals, fountains, and heroic statues.

In contrast to the formality and symmetry of the continental garden, the English arcadian landscape was a dramatic return to nature. Influenced by romantic landscape painting and the glory of ancient ruins, English garden designers in the eighteenth century sought to re-create a sense of nature's free, wild beauty. Instead of the classical elegance of geometric perspective, orderly planting beds, walkways, and rectangular reflecting pools, the English garden turned to poetic disorder, to free-form designs, even to reconstructed ruins and grottoes—in short, to the garden as a metaphor for romantic poetry and art. Its aim was the "picturesque."

"All gardening is landscape painting," remarked the first great English landscape designer, William Kent. It was Capability Brown and Humphry Repton, however, who created the arcadian landscapes of the great English country houses. In their designs the garden became landscape, a rolling vista that combined hills and fields, clumps of trees, rushing water, poetic lakes, and everywhere distant views. The flower garden was replaced by the beauties of landscape. There are "three aspects of landscape gardening," wrote William Shenstone, "the sublime, the beautiful, and the melancholy or pensive."

The "English garden" as we know it evolved from these poetic landscapes. The flower garden near the house made a comeback in the nineteenth century, replacing the vast green lawns just beyond the door. With a new emphasis on color and an abundance of what appeared to be (though not at all) disordered plantings in mixed species, the glorious flower beds that we think of as English became popular. This style of informal "cottage garden" swept into fashion and could be seen everywhere—from the terraces of grand houses of Britain to Monet's gardens at Giverny. The return of flower gardens and the Victorian interest in the exotic and the extravagant led to increasing use of imported plants, rare flowers, and "the gardenesque"—a deliberately near-chaotic approach to landscape.

To Americans, gifted with spectacular landscapes of a "natural paradise," most thoughts of French formality seemed irrelevant. As Americans first moved beyond their careful, colonial-style gardens into the realm of larger pleasure gardens, many were surely influenced by the English style. Americans with large estates, as well as those planning the first public parks, tried to incorporate natural landscape wonders into their own garden designs. Picturesque gardens were nestled into areas like the magnificent Palisades along the Hudson River, their dramatic settings adding to both design and ambience.

As the great era of wealth in the late nineteenth century brought increased travel abroad, America's new rich familiarized themselves with the elegant French and Italian landscape. Castles rivaling those of Europe were constructed in places like Newport and Philadelphia. Surrounding them were great formal gardens, patterned after Versailles or other grand continental wonders. To the owners of the American palaces, the French garden seemed the epitome of grandeur, the free-form English garden a less elegant option.

As you visit gardens today, you'll find distinct examples of both continental formality and the English "picturesque." But in many cases, particularly in gardens designed in the more recent past, you'll see a mixture of styles and influences that is typical of so many of our contemporary arts. Borrowing liberally from the varied ideas of the past, today's gardens might include formality and fountains as well as free-form planting beds and abstract contemporary sculpture. Exotic plantings, so prized by Victorians, might grow alongside a traditional Roman wall, or a geometric reflecting pool might be edged with contemporary tile. The postmodern emphasis on using elements from diverse sources has not escaped the world of landscape design. Thus, the debate between English informality and continental formality has all but passed into garden history, like the artificial grotto, the ha-ha, and the topiary maze.

The Colonial Garden

Let every house be placed if the Person pleases in the middle of its plot so that there may be found on each side for Gardens or Orchards, or fields, so that it may be a green Country Town . . . and will always be wholesome.

— WILLIAM PENN

COLONIAL GARDENS are an important part of America's cultural heritage, and one of its most delightful. Scattered about the East Coast, from New England to the South, they represent a particular time in our history. Whether authentic seventeenth- and eighteenth-century gardens, replicas, or simply newer interpretations of a basic style, they all share certain characteristics, with some variation. More formal than not (without being necessarily "grand"), they are ordered, geometric, and often symmetrical. Most are enclosed and intimate. Their organized structure reflects the needs and perspectives of a culture that prized order, balance, and economy.

The early settlers had a pragmatic approach to gardening, whether they were facing the harsh winters of upstate New York or the milder climate of Maryland. First, it was essential to enclose each household compound to keep out animals, wild or domestic. Within a fence or stone wall was a well-planned setup that emphasized function, rather than aesthetics, without compromising overall harmony and charm. The location of the house, its outbuildings and connecting "yards," and planted areas were carefully sited for best drainage and exposure. Each had its specific purpose. Between the house and outbuildings was the "dooryard," where animals were shorn, soap made, or wool dyed. This rustic spot was hardly a place for much greenery, except for a few shade trees (which were also useful as places to attach pulleys to lift heavy objects).

Each family maintained a basic garden and orchard to serve its needs. These formal plantings were often wedged in small areas between the house, yards, sheds, barns, meadows, and pastures. At first, necessity dictated planting vegetables and fruit shrubs and trees, rather than flowers. (During the eighteenth century, gardens became less utilitarian and often included decorative plants, as well as edibles.) Orchards contained large fruit trees, such as apples, but pears, peaches, apricots, and plums were arranged in borders or espaliers closer to the house. Herbs used for cooking were planted in simple, rectangular plots next to the house, or were sometimes mixed in with other plants. Physicians sometimes kept a "physic garden," or botanic garden, to provide the proper curative herbs for their patients.

On large colonial southern plantations, it was especially essential to create kitchen gardens and orchards, as the plantations were often isolated from towns and villages. Unlike New England, plentiful varieties of English plants thrived there. According to Robert Beverly, who in 1705 wrote *History of the Present State of Virginia*, "A Kitchen-Garden don't thrive better or faster in any part of the Universe than there. They have all the Culinary Plants that grow in England, and in far greater perfection, than in England."

Most colonial gardens were arranged in neat, rectangular blocks bordered by boxwood (especially in the South) or other decorative plants. Separating these geometric, cultivated areas were brick or stone paths. The more elaborate gardens might also include a central azalea path aligned with the main door of the house and leading to a vista, stone bench, or statue. On either side of the walk were raised plots (for better drainage), usually arranged in symmetrical fashion. While vegetables and small fruits were kept in designated areas, ornamental plants surrounded the more important walkways. Sometimes edible plants and flowers were mixed in together, creating formal geometric designs.

In New England, especially in the more elegant houses of Boston and Providence, it was common practice to cultivate a garden in front of the house as well as in back. These tiny "parlor gardens" were sometimes no wider than the house itself and featured decorative shrubs and flowers.

During the eighteenth century, Philadelphia became one of the most important garden centers in the country. No doubt this was because of the Quakers' interest in botany and horticulture—not surprising in view of the fact that their austere lifestyle excluded most other arts and activities. The great horticulturist John Bartram, a Quaker who founded the first botanical garden in the colonies, was largely responsible for generating great interest in plants and gardens.

The results of his efforts are still very evident in the historic colonial gardens found in the Philadelphia region.

In Virginia and other parts of the South, colonial gardens tended to be larger and more elaborate than in the North. With the large-scale introduction of slavery into the southern colonies, manor houses were built, surrounded by often grand landscaped settings. One such place is the Governor's Place in Williamsburg, reputed for its elegant eighteenth-century gardens (and a popular tourist attraction to this day). Another is Gunston Hall, an example of a well-designed twentieth-century re-creation featuring a stately arrangement of boxwoods growing in neat, geometric hedges.

Thomas Jefferson, who along with George Washington was one of the most famous colonial gardeners of all, had an abiding interest in horticulture, garden design, and botany—and a fundamental belief that the strength of the country lay in its agrarian society. He surrounded his extraordinary estate, Monticello, with vegetable plots (where he conducted various experiments), flower beds, and orchards. Monticello and Washington's Mount Vernon are examples of the colonial style at its grandest; but, still, they were created in basically the same spirit as the simplest colonial garden, emphasizing the order, harmony, and balance of pleasure and usefulness.

The Walled Garden

> A Garden is my sister, my spouse; a spring shut up, a fountain sealed. Thy plants are an orchard of pomegranates with pleasant fruits.
>
> —SONG OF SOLOMON

THROUGHOUT HISTORY gardens have been seen as different, idealized worlds in which we create an orderly and beautiful environment cut off from tumultuous reality. Thus, of course, they

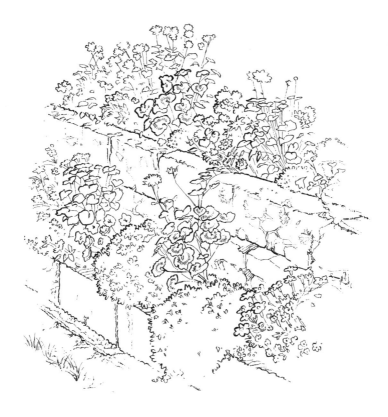

must be enclosed. Most gardens, in fact, are surrounded in some way—separated from the wild, the urban, the public, the unknown. In this way gardens are like beautifully framed paintings. Such divisions between the wild and intrusive, and the cultivated and the private, create the sense of specialness and secrecy that characterizes an enclosed space. The "secret garden" is a concept that is undeniably inviting.

Artificial boundaries for gardens—when they are not naturally surrounded by geographical borders—are most often created by walls, hedges, or fences. Whether the border is formed by high boxwood hedges or medieval stone walls, trellis fences, or rows of evergreens, the "framing" of the garden is found all over the world, and throughout garden history.

The walled garden is the most private, for walls—whether of stone or hedge—can be high and impenetrable. Their origins are long in the past, when they kept out human and animal intruders and protected those within. In many cultures the enclosed garden, designed for both useful growing and pleasing contemplation, was a practical or an aesthetic choice. But the enclosed gardens of some civilizations—such as Egyptian and medieval Christian—were also metaphors for religious belief. (Walled gardens of the Middle Ages, for example, were thought to symbolize freedom and beauty with precisely set boundaries.)

Beautiful enclosed gardens can be seen in paintings from Egyptian and Roman walls, in Persian miniatures, and in the cloisters of medieval buildings. Trellis-fenced gardens appear in Renaissance art; the great classical gardens of France and England used both hedges and fences to enclose parts of their elaborate landscape designs. Boxwood, evergreen, and other living borders were common in gardens ranging from ancient Rome to colonial America, their carefully tended shapes creating dense hedgerows and geometric patterns.

Many of these garden boundaries were not just utilitarian borders to surround the plantings, but were integral parts of the garden design. Medieval walls featured carvings, patterned stonework, delicate espaliered trees or climbing plants, and carved stone blossoms reflecting the blooms within the garden. Some of the thick hedge borders of the most complex European gardens were cut into topiary designs, making the garden "walls" fantastic in shape and illusion.

American enclosed gardens date to colonial times, when their walls kept out the frightening wilderness. Many early American gardens have high brick walls and matching paths whose subtle deep red contrasts delightfully with the dark shiny greens of ivy and boxwood. Versions in the United States of European cloisters and

Victorian "cottages" included walled gardens. Our great nineteenth-century estates include many enclosed garden areas, in which marble and granite not only provide a backdrop for plantings and sculpture, but create both color and texture in themselves. Espaliered fruit trees, climbing roses, ivies, wisteria, and trumpet vines are among the many popular plantings that can be seen covering the walls of enclosed gardens in the Mid-Atlantic.

Today the walled garden is often in the middle of a city. Urban gardeners use stone or brick walls in imaginative and contemporary ways, sometimes combining sculpture, falling water, and environmental design. Some of the smallest but most appealing walled gardens today are the "vest-pocket" parks in our cities.

Clearly, the concept of the enclosed garden is still valid; its plantings and design may be symbolic or practical or purely aesthetic, but the walled garden remains the special, magical space, serene and cut off from the world outside.

The Topiary Garden

> And all these [flowers] by the skill of your Gardener,
> so comelily and orderly placed in your borders and
> squares and so intermingled, that one looking thereon,
> cannot but wonder to see, what Nature, corrected by
> Art, can do.
>
> — WILLIAM LAWSON
> *A New Orchard and Garden*, 1618

*T*OPIARY, the ancient art of shaping plants into living sculptures, has brought charm, whimsy, and surprise to many a garden over the centuries. The term comes from the Latin *toparius*, referring to a gardener who specializes in carving plants; for it is such a gardener who, with the skill and vision of an artist, can transform an ordinary

landscape into a delightful living tableau, adding both elegance and fun to the landscape. Because of its many possibilities of expression, topiary art has appealed to gardeners of all kinds, including the most eccentric, who find it an amusing outlet for their imaginations.

The topiary tradition comes with a wealth of sculpted plant shapes and designs. Shrubs and trees are pruned, clipped, cut, coaxed, and styled (sometimes on wire frames) into fanciful animals, mythological creatures, or elegant geometric forms. Yew, privet, hemlock, boxwood, and ivy—to name some of the most popular plants used—can be fashioned into peacocks, roosters, dragons, and centaurs, as well as pyramids, gloves, arches, and decorative scalloped hedges. Some topiary gardens feature entire sequential scenes: for example, a leafy foxhunt or a flotilla of ships. Others are created on an intimate scale and might include potted topiary that can be moved about or brought indoors.

Topiary gardens are not limited to green sculptures, however. There are also espalier gardens, knot gardens, parterres, and mazes. The espalier is a plant trained into an open, flat pattern to create a two-dimensional effect. The branches of shrubs and trees—often fruit trees such as pear, peach, and apple trees—are bent and pruned into intricate, delicate motifs to adorn walls and other vertical surfaces.

Knot gardens are level beds whose designs are made from the intertwining patterns of herbs and hedges. (Today's versions sometimes include flowers and pebbles as well.)

The parterre (French for "on the ground") is a variation of the knot garden. Usually on a larger scale, its designs are more fluid, with arabesques, open scrolls, or fleur-de-lis. Patterns are created by using carefully clipped dwarf hedges, flowers, grass, and colored stones.

The maze—one of the more delightful topiary forms—is like a lifesize puzzle. It is made of a network of connecting hedges and paths intended to amuse through surprise and confusion. In its earlier forms, in eighteenth-century Europe, the maze sometimes included hidden water games and sprays that were meant to catch the unsuspecting visitor by surprise, or well-hidden lovers' benches at the very center.

The history of topiary gardens shows us that though they were highly popular from Roman times until the eighteenth century, they are much more rare in contemporary gardens (though in European gardens of the past you will find many restored topiaries).

The earliest recorded topiary garden seems to have come about in ancient Rome. Around A.D. 100 the younger Pliny drew a distinction between the beauties of nature—beloved by the Romans—and the beauties of a cultivated garden. Pliny wrote long letters describing the gardens he had laid out at his Tuscan estate. Distinguishing between art and nature, he commented that the beauty of the landscape was owing to nature, while the beauty of his garden was owed to "art."

In describing in detail his plantings and garden design, Pliny indicated that his gardeners had employed what we know of today as topiary gardens. His paths, he wrote, were lined with boxwood hedges "and in between grass plots with box trees cut into all kinds of different shapes, some of them being letters spelling out the name of the owner or of the gardener who did the work." Interspersed with these topiary delights were white marble statues, obelisks, pillars, and seating areas.

A friend of emperor Augustus named C. Matius was responsible for the invention of the topiary garden. Matius, according to Pliny's uncle, had invented the cutting of trees into various shapes around 5 B.C. (Don't be surprised by the sophistication of ancient Roman gardeners; they had been grafting fruit trees, for example, for generations by the time Pliny made his gardens!)

We next hear of the topiary garden in medieval times, when the Flemish, in particular, favored small clipped evergreens (box or yew, as today) trained into tiers. (You can see a somewhat later example of the Flemish topiary in Pieter Brueghel's painting *Spring*.) But unlike the Romans, the Flemish apparently only clipped their evergreens in simple ways, rather than in the elaborate designs described by Pliny.

French medieval gardeners developed the espalier in their walled cities, where there was little room for orchards. The fact that espaliers required little space and that they bore their fruit early and abundantly was a great asset during those harsh times. Later espaliers became popular as purely ornamental features in French gardens.

(Also developed in France in the Middle Ages, by the way, were the first mazes: They were inspired by the medieval belief that a penitent soul might crawl on his hands and knees to imitate the path of earthly travail and thus gain heavenly grace.)

Topiary art came thoroughly into fashion in the Italian Renaissance, when all of the arts and their illusionary qualities were so admired, and when so many classical and ancient styles were revived. A "Renaissance" gentleman named Leon Battista Alberti described the principles of garden design in the fifteenth century.

Among his many pieces of advice (on a wide range of architectural and landscaping subjects) was to select sites with "a view of cities, land and sea, a spreading plain, and the known peaks of the hills and mountains." He recommended cool shell-covered grottoes, groves of fruit trees, and box-bordered paths and topiary work. "The gardeners of ancient times," he said, "flattered their patrons by writing their names in letters formed in box and other odorous herbs." We can see examples of the elaborate gardens of the fifteenth and sixteenth centuries (such as those described by Alberti) in engravings and paintings from France and Italy and England.

In fact, in Queen Elizabeth the First's England of the sixteenth century, topiary designs, knot gardens, and mazes became quite fashionable at the palaces and castles of the aristocracy. At Sudely Castle in Gloucestershire, topiary yew hedges included small, doorlike openings for sheltering during England's sudden and frequent rainstorms, and Elizabeth's hunting lodge had both a knot garden and flat-cut hedges that are said to have been used for drying "linen, cloathes and yarne"! Among the designs used in Elizabethan gardens were "cockle shells," "beestes," "men armed in the field, ready to give battle," "swift-running grey-hounds," "pretty pyramides," and "little turrets with bellies." Later English gardens featured "outdoor rooms" in which the lawn was the carpet and the topiary the furniture.

France became a center of formal gardens under the Bourbon kings. In the seventeenth century, the art of topiary was apparently de rigueur in the great formal settings of the French châteaus. Extravaganzas of all kinds characterized French baroque court life; not the least of them were the elaborate pavilions and topiary designs. These included living plant decorations in the shapes of animals and people, sailing ships, and birds, as well as complex arrangements based on medieval dance patterns, parterres, three-part patterns, crisscrossed walks, mazes, and other features to entertain the lords and ladies who strolled through them.

But the craze for topiary gardens came to an end. In 1728 a French garden architect and writer (Alexandre Le Blond) wrote disparagingly, "At present nobody gives into these trifles [topiary gardens] in France, how well so ever they may be kept. . . . We chose rather a plain regularity less clutter'd and confus'd, which indeed looks much more noble and great." Rousseau's dedication to the principles of naturalism and informality and "the simple life" added to the dislike for the artificial topiary design. Instead a new emphasis on natural beauty replaced the intricate formal gardens of the baroque.

Visits to stately homes of Britain and châteaus of France will still often include historic topiary gardens and mazes. But in the United States, where we do not have the tradition in our past, they are more of a rarity. However, we have found several for your enjoyment. Read on!

The Conservatory Garden

There is an inherent wonderful fascination in being able, in the middle of winter, to open the window of a salon and feel a balmy spring breeze instead of the raw December or January air. It may be raining outside, or the snow may be falling in soft flakes from a black sky, but one opens the glass doors and finds oneself in an earthly paradise that makes fun of the wintry showers.

— Princess Mathilde de Bonaparte, 1869

THE IDEA OF collecting, nurturing, and displaying plants in an enclosed, controlled environment is an ancient one. The first greenhouses may have been built by the Romans to protect the exotic plants they found during their military campaigns in distant lands. The emperor Nero's *specularium* (for so this type of Roman

structure was called) contained his much loved cucumbers, which he could thus enjoy throughout the year. Over the course of human history, plants have been gathered, arranged, and housed for many reasons—from the most pragmatic to aesthetic, spiritual, scientific, or even whimsical. And their artificial habitats—from the specularium to the conservatory—have evolved considerably.

The earliest indoor gardens functioned both as places to display plants and to store and protect them from the sometimes harsh European winters. Ornamental plants were admired and often regarded as "trophies" won during victorious battles. (The taste for unusual flora existed at least as far back as ancient Egypt, when royal gardeners were routinely sent to other countries to gather rare species.) Crusaders and later many explorers came home with unfamiliar varieties, which required careful tending in controlled environments.

In sixteenth-century England and France, it became fashionable to maintain decorative citrus trees, and "orangeries" came into being. In the elegant estates of the time, these winter gardens were de rigueur. During the coldest months, orange and lemon trees in large tubs were placed in neat rows inside glass-walled chambers, mostly for show. Some were on a very grand scale; indeed, the 9,000-square-foot orangerie at Heidelberg Castle in 1619 included more than 400 trees, many of which were at least 25 feet high!

But the real "botanic" gardens filled with rare plants—both indoor and outdoor—came into being as a result of a new interest in the spiritual and scientific dimensions of the plant kingdom. The garden of Eden was actually the inspiration for the botanic gardens of the sixteenth century. After the discovery of the New World's natural life, the first notion arose of a *hortus inculsis,* a gathering of all the plants that had been dispersed from that Biblical paradise. Exotic plants brought back from voyages around the world formed the basis for the first botanic gardens at Leiden, Padua, and Montpellier. In the next century, others were started in Paris, London, and Uppsala, Sweden.

Most of these early gardens were arranged in squares, divided into quadrants representing the four corners of the earth (in those days that meant Asia, Africa, Europe, and America). The quadrants were then divided into parterres, with grass walks dividing them. Each plant was carefully labeled; the botanic garden became a "living encyclopedia" of Creation. (It was believed, in fact, that the visitor who spent time contemplating in such a place might regain his or her lost innocence and even gain insight into the "mind of God.")

By the seventeenth century, theologians upset this easy method of finding paradise. (They looked at zoos—established for the same reason—and saw no peaceable kingdoms ensuing.) Some great thinkers believed that the natural wilderness was closer to the original than these highly organized settings. And there were problems of a more practical nature: Which climate did the garden of Eden have? Plants from so many different climes could not grow in the same place at the same temperature. The botanic garden as a place of science was created; it featured indoor and outdoor areas devoted to climactic differences, propagation, and the survival of species.

In their capacity as "laboratories" for scientific study, botanic gardens and, particularly, greenhouses, became places to grow plants for medicinal purposes. During the seventeenth and eighteenth centuries, botanists traveled to the New World on merchant ships to identify and gather species of possible medicinal or other scientific value. John Bartram, among the most famous of these botanists, discovered many valuable tropical plants in his scientific expeditions abroad. (He was, by the way, a member of Capt. James Cook's scientific expedition in 1772.)

The emphasis on greenhouses and imported rarities from all over the world also had an artistic effect: the concept of a "museum" of plants. The early botanic garden became a collection of exotic and fascinating individual plants, set out for easy enjoyment and identification, rather than a larger, overall form of environmental or artistic beauty. (As we will see, these diverse aims have been admirably united in the botanic gardens of today.)

One of the first great botanical gardens in the United States was in New York City, where Rockefeller Center is today; the Elgin Botanic Garden was started in 1801. A huge area with a conservatory featured scientifically identified plants. The garden—then in "the wilds" of upper Manhattan—was surrounded by a belt of trees and a great stone wall. Needless to say, it did not survive the city's expansion.

But in 1824 a Belgian horticulturalist named André Parmentier came to New York and built the Brooklyn Botanic Garden. One of its most popular aspects was a tower from which visitors could see the gardens and surrounding area with a bird's-eye view. Parmentier's wonderful gardens still exist today and can be visited.

Another such enterprise was begun only twenty-nine years after Washington, D.C., became the capital of the United States (in 1820), when a group of amateur scientists founded a similar enterprise there. Although the garden lasted for only about eighteen years before it ran out of funds, the idea of a national botanic garden was taken up again in 1842.

Plans for a new garden were encouraged by the 1838–42 commercial expedition of Capt. Charles Wilkes (the model for Captain Ahab, by the way). He had circumnavigated the globe with 440 men and six ships (one of which must have been needed just to carry home the 10,000 plant variety seeds, dried samples, and live plants he collected from all over the world!). A federally funded national botanic garden was finally built in 1842. In 1849 it was moved to its present location and it can be visited today in all its splendor.

As indoor gardens have had a variety of functions over the ages, so too have they evolved stylistically. The earliest greenhouses contained little glass; indeed, it is likely that Romans used sheets of mica instead to allow the sun to filter in. With improved technology, particularly during the industrial age, greenhouses became all-glass structures and took on new shapes. While eighteenth-century orangeries and conservatories had had extensive windows but conventional roofs, in the nineteenth century they began to be built with domed roofs. Theorists had discovered that the form of roof best suited for the admission of the sun's rays was hemispherical. Because of the development of iron frames and glazed roofs, it was now possible to build greenhouses that looked like what we now think of as "conservatories" (and what we imagine when we inevitably read about them in Victorian novels). These elegant and fanciful structures culminated with Sir Joseph Paxton's famous

Crystal Palace, inaugurated as the main attraction at the First International Exhibition in London's Hyde Park in 1851. Greeted with great enthusiasm, its enormous success helped stimulate the building of conservatories everywhere, including in America. More elaborate than greenhouses, conservatories contained plants primarily chosen for their showy effect.

The Water Garden

> Any garden ornament or piece of architecture mirrored in water receives an addition to its dignity by the repetition and continuation of upright line.
> —GERTRUDE JEKYLL, 1901

WATER HAS embellished gardens around the world since the earliest civilizations. It has been used in gardens not only for practical reasons but also for pure pleasure and decoration. The effects of water on the senses are varied and fascinating: Water can delight,

charm, soothe, cool, stimulate, and excite. Through its magical powers of illusion, and reflection, it can create an environment of mystery and even surprise. Natural sources of water—streams, brooks, or waterfalls—as well as artful canals, pools, or fountains have been focal points in gardens over the ages.

The Egyptians were among the first who recognized the importance of "decorative water" in garden design. Ancient tomb paintings depict gardens with rectangular pools, lilies, lotus, and papyrus. Not only were these basins of water practical—they were used to irrigate the surroundings—but they were also refreshingly appealing in the parched lands.

The pleasure-loving Romans copied these early models in their own gardens, adding more sophisticated elements, such as elaborate fountains and canals. The fabled garden of Pliny the Younger included (according to his nephew) "a semicircular bench of white marble shaded with a vine which is trained on four small pillars of marble. Water, gushing through several little pipes from under this bench . . . falls onto a stone cistern underneath, from whence it is received into a fine polished marble basin, so artfully contrived that it is always full without overflowing." It seems that at mealtime, plates of food were placed on the water so they could float from one person to the next.

Water, revered by the Persians as the essence of life, was the chief element in their paradise gardens. These magnificent, enclosed oases with fountains, tiled pools, and intricate water channels provided a delicious respite in a torrid climate. Formal and geometric, they usually included rows of stately cypress trees and scented roses, irrigated by underground tunnels.

Water gardens reached some of their highest levels of artistry in those created by the Moors of medieval Spain. Such magnificent and lavish gardens as those in the Alhambra were intricately planned by some of the most sophisticated designers of all time.

These masterful hydraulic engineers/artists used ingenious techniques to channel precious water from distant mountain springs through elaborate tunnels to palaces and courtyards. The gardens were thus filled with the sight and sound of water continuously flowing (and recycled) through fountains, marbled channels, and basins.

The rest of Europe (which during the Middle Ages had confined its gardens to relatively modest cloisters with small wells and fountains) saw a rebirth of the water garden during the Renaissance, especially in Italy. Along with a renewed interest in antiquities came a fascination with science and the study of such basic elements as water; water became a central focus of Italian villa gardens. Amidst the waters of elegant fountains and graceful pools, and even inside mysterious grottoes, Italian designers placed statues depicting mythological characters—ranging from river gods and gorgons to Venus and Neptune surrounded by nymphs and dolphins. Amazing waterpowered machines and animated ornaments graced some villa gardens. The fabled Villa d'Este, one of the most dazzling water gardens of all time (it still delights visitors today), displayed spectacular aquatic fireworks in addition to its other exquisite garden features.

Fountains were used most lavishly in seventeenth-century French gardens. At Versailles, for example, the master designer André Le Nôtre (along with an army of artists and engineers) channeled water through myriad dams, falls, pools, cascades, and an especially long canal (where mock naval battles were occasionally held to amuse the courtiers). Le Nôtre's designs for Versailles became a standard by which numerous other formal gardens were (and are still) measured.

Romantic English gardens used water in a less artificial way. Instead of the grand geometric, formal pools, and fountains of the French, they featured meandering streams and rivers surrounded with naturalistic plantings and graceful garden paths. Some of the great Capability Brown's designs called for picturesque garden lakes, created by dammed streams and massive excavations.

Of course, the "natural" use of water—so favored in the romantic era—had long been featured in the gardens of the Far East. In classical Chinese and Japanese gardens, water, regarded as a vital ingredient, appeared almost always in an entirely naturalistic way. But water in Asian gardens also had symbolic significance; for example, both the sight and the sound of water in Japanese gardens is part of the aesthetic importance of their traditional gardens. (See the remarks about Asian gardens.)

Today water gardens have been inspired by these varied historic and cultural traditions and reinterpreted to accommodate contemporary needs and tastes. As you visit gardens that feature water designs, you will perhaps identify some of these stylistic elements.

The Rock Garden

> It may appear at first that the collection of stones etc. is designed to appear wild and irregular, little Art would be required in its construction; but this is so far from being the case, that perhaps rockwork is more difficult to design and execute than any other kind of garden scenery.
>
> —JANE LOUDON, CA. 1930

WE TAKE rock gardens for granted nowadays, enjoying the combination of hard, surprising stone and delicate, careful plantings. Many a rocky American hillside is planted these days with wildflowers and alpine specialties, and some such gardens are even created from the start.

But the rock garden does not have as long a history as most of the designs and styles of gardens we describe. In fact, the rock garden dates to 1777, when Sir Joseph Banks, a British naturalist (and president of the Royal Society some years later), visited Iceland. On a twelve-day hike to a volcanic mountain in Iceland, Banks collected the lava from the volcano's last eruption five years earlier. (He used it for ballast for his ship on the return to Britain.)

When he got home, he presented the hardened lava to the Chelsea Physic Garden, where it was combined with piles of stone from the old walls of the Tower of London, discarded bricks, and various other types of stone. Plants began to grow all over this huge and motley mound of rock.

Within fifty years, rock gardens were popular in Britain. Jane and John Loudon, noted writers on all subjects of gardening, described "rockwork" as fragments of rock "thrown together in an artistic manner, so as to produce a striking and pleasing effect, and to serve as a nest or repository" for a variety of plants. Rock gardens are more difficult to design than they look, they warned their readers. As the "cluttered" garden (much like the Victorian parlor) soon replaced

the expansive, airy stretches of the previous era, the rock garden with its many composite parts became more and more popular.

Among the early designs in private gardens for rockeries, as they were known, were an imitation Swiss mountain scene made of white marble to simulate snow, and a naturalistic rocky hollow made from an abandoned quarry. Plants for these original gardens varied from traditional British ornamental shrubs and flowers to imported specimens, originating from rocky hillsides in other countries.

By midcentury many English rock gardens were devoted entirely to alpine plants in the Swiss style, even though the plants' native habitat on high, snowy mountains could not easily be transplanted to Britain. Advice proliferated on caring for such plants—described as "low, bushy, and evergreen" and "tiny and elfin"—and on how to design the rockeries. Before long, the rock garden became synonymous with the alpine garden and a fashionable addition to many a country estate, where miniature mountains, gorges, valleys, waterfalls, and bridges appeared.

The alpine garden was the subject of intense interest to botanists and gardeners who traveled the world in search of rare plants that adapted well to their stony surroundings. The designs for such gardens were described by Reginald Farrer in My Rock Garden. He wrote derisively that there were three common ideas for rock gardens: the "Almond Pudding scheme," which has spiky pinnacles of limestone jutting up among the plants; the "Dog's Grave," with a pudding shape but its stones laid flat; and the "Devil's Lapful," which contains cartloads of bald, square-faced boulders dropped about anywhere, with plants dropped in between them. He preferred a naturalistic setting. (And so did many later garden designers, who went so far as to use imitation rocks to create "lifelike" landscapes.)

Today the alpine idea is still popular, but it is no longer an imitative or confining design. There is great freedom of idea and layout in the American rock gardens we have visited. Many combine the naturalistic features of a rocky terrain (with the huge boulders common to our part of the world) and a judicious use of stone walls and stairways and other rocky additions. The plantings in these gardens range widely from imported alpine delicacies to plants that lend themselves to falling over stone walls. Raised beds, stone pools, and tiny waterfalls are among the elements you might find.

The Asian Garden

> A lonely pond in age-old stillness sleeps,
> Apart, unstirred by sound or motion till
> Suddenly into it a little frog leaps . . .
>
> —BASHO (1644–94)

GARDENS OF the Orient were the first to become living artistic statements. Closely aligned with religious beliefs of Buddhism, Taoism, and Shintoism, Chinese and Japanese gardens were places of meditation and renewal. In an attempt to tame nature's wildness, deliberately placed trees and plants were combined with materials of long-lasting value, like wood, sand, and stone. Each element of the garden was symbolic, designed for spiritual awareness as its owners strolled through it.

Chinese "cup gardens"—ranging in size from picturesque lakes surrounded by hills to small stone areas with a bonsai (artificially pruned, miniature tree) in the center—were among the first symbolically designed Asian gardens. The earliest cup garden is believed to have been created by the great landscape painter and poet Wang Wei (A.D. 699–759) during the T'ang dynasty. It was Wang Wei who first articulated the close relationship of the Chinese garden to art, poetry, and spirituality.

If you look at a traditional scroll painting of a Chinese landscape, in fact, it is hard to know which art is imitating which. For

the great Chinese gardens have the ambience of paintings, while the paintings seem inextricably bound up with the delicately designed traditional garden. Harmonious in design, the Chinese landscape is distinctive, with its careful balance of leaning trees and craggy rocks, arched bridges over reflective water, and gentle flowering plants.

The cup garden was surrounded (like the inside of a cup) by a wall, hedge, or other barrier in order to provide isolation from the chaos of the outside world. Within its boundaries, the cup garden drew the visitor's attention to accents—a particular plant or stone or body of water. The garden's purpose was introspection and privacy, using an artistic design and symbolism to bring close communication and union with nature and its forces.

The symbolic elements and design of ancient Chinese gardens strongly influenced the Japanese, who went on to create elaborate and exquisite gardens of their own. The Japanese stroll garden also became a place for introspection: an orderly, aesthetic environment where balance, beauty, and harmony mirrored the proper harmony of the soul.

There is little that is accidental or uncalculated in a Japanese garden. Carefully placed, asymmetrical plantings—such as bamboo and katsura trees, ferns, delicate iris, or lilies—grow among symbolic settings. These important elements range from free-form ponds that reflect the sky, to statuary such as small deities or cranes (representing wisdom and long life), to raked sand (representing the ocean's tides), to carefully placed rocks and small stones (suggesting the earth's natural forms), to tiny islands in the pond (symbolizing clouds). Small buildings such as the familiar Japanese teahouse provide a haven of peace and beauty. To the Shintoists, spirits inhabit all natural phenomena, and the Japanese garden suggests no less than heaven on earth.

Southeast Asian gardens share many of the same designs and ideas, but in Thailand and Burma, for example, there is greater freedom from the precise symbolism of the Japanese. Though not as burdened by the meaning of each rock and bamboo shoot, these gardens are also spiritual sanctuaries adorned with sculptured deities, including small Buddhas set amid the greenery and flowers.

The Asian garden stunned and delighted Westerners who traveled to the East. In the seventeenth and eighteenth centuries, many aspects of Chinese artistry—including garden design and exotic plants—began to appear in European gardens and subsequently in America.

Today, in addition to many great Chinese and Japanese gardens carefully maintained in the United States, we also find Oriental plantings and landscape design intermixed with the more Western styles of many of our American gardens. Among the elements adopted in our own gardens are numerous exotic trees (ranging from

Asian magnolias and rhododendrons to Japanese flowering cherries) and many flowers, including species of jasmine, poppies, azaleas, and lilies.

But even more obvious to our Western eyes are the elements of Asian design that have crept into our own formal and informal gardens: trickling water and delicate lily ponds, small arched bridges and waterfalls, "living still lifes of stones and foliage so prized in Asian design, and garden areas created for meditation and harmony with nature."

Gardenwalks in Delaware

After all, what is a garden for? It is for "delight," for "sweet solace," for "the purest of all human pleasures; the greatest refreshment of the spirits of men"; it is to promote "jucunditie of minde"; it is to "call home over-wearied spirits." So say the old writers, and we cannot amend their words, which will stand as long as there are gardens on earth and people to love them.

—GERTRUDE JEKYLL

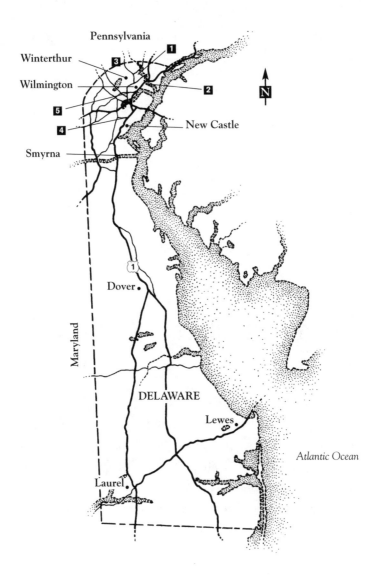

1. Wilmington: Nemours Mansion and Gardens
2. Wilmington: Rockwood Gardens
3. Winterthur: Winterthur

Don't Miss . . .

4. New Castle: The George Read II House and Garden
5. Wilmington: Hagley Museum and Library

1. Nemours Mansion and Gardens

P.O. Box 109, Rockland Road, **Wilmington,** DE 19899;
(302) 651–6912; www.nemours.org/no/mansion

*N*EMOURS NEEDS little introduction. One of the best-known and most often visited country estates on the East Coast, it is also one of the most opulent, with its sumptuous 102-room mansion, formal gardens, and acres of woodlands. Situated in the picturesque Brandywine landscape, it is reminiscent of a French château.

In fact, Versailles was the inspiration, at least for the extraordinary gardens. Extending neatly in a sweeping axis from the house to a Temple of Love, the gardens include elegant fountains, pools, urns, statuary, an intricate parterre, colonnades, tree-lined allées, a maze, a sunken garden—and vistas at every turn. Everything is on a grand scale, from the one-acre reflecting pool with its 157 water jets (though not in perpetual motion), to the massive limestone colonnade, to an extravaganza of sculptures against a marble wall, to the 800 feet of flowering borders enclosing one of the gardens.

Nemours (named after an ancestral town in France) was built between 1909 and 1910 by Alfred I. duPont, though the gardens themselves were not completed until 1932. His goal was to reproduce a version of Versailles, the ultimate in splendor (unlike his du Pont cousins, who were creating nearby Longwood and Winterthur on a more modest scale). In addition to overseeing the dramatic garden design, he concerned himself with such details as the designs of the tree boxes on the terrace, which are like those that held thousands of orange trees at Versailles.

If you stretch your imagination a bit and try to disregard the crowds and modern-day tourist amenities, you will find that coming to Nemours is almost like stepping back into seventeenth-century France. Unfortunately, guided tours of the mansion and gardens are par for the course (and reservations are necessary), limiting your freedom to wander about at will, at your own pace.

❀ **Admission:** Fee.

Garden open: Tuesday through Sunday from May to November. Tours are offered at 9:00 A.M., 11:00 A.M., 1:00 P.M., and 3:00 P.M. on all days except Sunday, when there is no 9:00 A.M. tour.

Further information: Guided tours (for a minimum of two hours) include the mansion and a bus ride through the gardens. You may also see some of the gardens on foot if you make arrangements with the bus driver. For reservations you can phone or write. No children under sixteen are allowed.

Directions: From Philadelphia take Interstate 95 south to exit 8 (Route 202). Go north, turn left at the third light (Route 141); go two more lights and turn left onto Rockland Road. You will see a long stone wall surrounding the adjacent Alfred I. duPont Institute. Park at the end of the stone wall. The reception area is located at the parking lot.

2. Rockwood Gardens

Shipley Road, **Wilmington,** DE; (302) 761–4340;
www.rockwood.org

ARDENESQUE" is a term that aptly describes this estate's landscape. Surrounding a rather gloomy but impressive mid-nineteenth-century Rural Gothic mansion (with a delectable attached conservatory), these grounds are designed as a pleasurable retreat. Here you'll find many exotic trees from the Orient and around the world, expansive lawns, a walled rose garden, and numerous other country delights. The estate covers a rather rolling terrain and overlooks the Delaware River (though in most places the view is overgrown nowadays). You can be guided through the grounds or tour by yourself, map in hand.

The house, built in 1850 by merchant banker Joseph Shipley, is interestingly furnished with all kinds of antiques, and, in keeping with the period design, has many windows with views of the gardens. Best of all, there is a small but wonderfully sumptuous high-ceilinged conservatory, where rarities and tropical plantings—orange and lemon trees, great ferns, orchids—grow all around you and overhead. The oldest standing greenhouse in the nation, this glass construction has a truly Victorian ambience.

Outdoors you walk across vast lawns with great trees—we were particularly delighted by the gnarled, curving shapes of the monkey puzzle trees that contrast with the tall spires of giant hemlocks and larches. (Such design elements are part of the plan in gardenesque design.) You will encounter a low stone wall all around the gardens; this is called the ha-ha, a structure beloved by English novelists. (It is simply a pretty way to keep cattle out of the front yard.)

Also reminiscent of the Victorian English country estate are the pleasure gardens; the walled, onetime kitchen garden that contains boxwood hedges and little walkways outlining pleasantly overgrown plantings; and a 1911 rose garden featuring rambling roses in white, pink, and mauve in summer. In other seasons you'll also enjoy Rockwood: The spectacular autumn foliage colors, the pinetum in its winter beauty, and rhododendrons flowering in spring all make this a nice year-round destination.

✿ **Admission:** Free.

Garden open: Tuesday through Sunday 7:00 A.M. to 7:00 P.M.; closed on major holidays.

Further information: Tours are offered from 10:00 A.M. to 3:00 P.M.

Directions: From Wilmington take I–95 north to exit 9 (Marsh Road). Turn right onto Marsh Road and right again at the first light onto Washington Street Extension. Make another right at the first light at Shipley Road. Rockwood's driveway is the first on your left.

3. Winterthur

Route 52 (Kennett Pike), **Winterthur,** DE;
(302) 888–4600, (800) 448–3883; www.winterthur.org

*W*INTERTHUR, along with the other du Pont estates that dot the picturesque Brandywine region, is grand and vast, as you might expect. What comes as a surprise—and a welcome one, at that—is the style of its gardens. Naturalistic and free flowing, they are very different from the formal environments traditionally associated with comparable mansions, such as nearby Nemours or Longwood. Set in an idyllic landscape of rolling hills, meadows, ponds, and forests, they are understandably among the most popular gardens in the country.

Apparently Henry Francis du Pont, creator of Winterthur's gardens, museum, and library, had two great passions in life: collecting American antiques and gardening. His mansion is now a prestigious museum housing one of the best collections of American decorative arts anywhere; surrounding it are nearly 1,000 acres, including eleven main planted areas that testify to his great love of gardens.

The property, a working farm until 1951, was named after an ancestral site in Switzerland. When first purchased by the family in 1837, it was a 450-acre estate with a twelve-room Greek revival house. By 1925 it had evolved into a much more elaborate setup, including dairy and poultry farms; flower and vegetable gardens; a golf course, sawmill, and railroad station—even a post office. But it was Winterthur's fifth owner, Henry du Pont, whose energy and imagination made it what it is today.

From 1926, when he inherited the property, to 1951, when it opened to the public, du Pont further developed and expanded the farmland and gardens. Committed to maintaining Winterthur's peaceful parklike ambience, he engaged an old family friend, landscape architect Marian Coffin, to create naturalistic planted areas that would blend seamlessly with the landscape. As a dedicated and knowledgeable plantsman (he himself had studied horticulture at Harvard), du Pont selected a vast assortment of species from around the world to enhance the natural setting. He was particularly fond of azaleas, rhododendrons, dogwoods, and quinces, whose colors he chose with an artistic eye. With the help of an impressive staff of gardeners, he planned and supervised the blooming sequence of his flowers and shrubs with the utmost precision, so that the season could last as long as possible. To add idyllic charm, du Pont even created four ponds (now home to assorted ducks and geese) from the existing Clenny Run.

The resulting gardens can be viewed by foot or—for those who would rather not walk up and down the hilly terrain—by tram, a delightful experience in itself. From April through October the gardens unfold like a series of tableaux, with subtle changes in color and fragrance, from the earliest daffodils and azaleas to autumn's brilliant shades. Among the offerings are the Azalea Woods, an eight-acre wonderland of rhododendrons, azaleas, ferns, wildflowers, and shrubs beneath towering white oaks and tulip poplars; Magnolia Bend, a spring-fresh combination of pale pink and deep red blossoms; March Bank (dating from 1902, making it the oldest planted area), a glorious hillside of naturalized daffodils, snowdrops, crocus, and glory-of-the-snow; the Quarry Garden (du Pont's last creation), an unusual rock garden made within an abandoned quarry; and the Winter Hazel Area, a proliferation of color that should not be missed in April. Marian Coffin designed three main areas: the Peony Garden and the only two formal gardens at Winterthur, the Sundial Garden (where fragrant plants are arranged in circles around an antique bronze sundial) and the intimate Reflecting Pool, one of our favorite spots.

When du Pont enlarged his mansion in 1929, he wanted an attached garden that would make an inviting transition from house to surrounding landscape. The Reflecting Pool was inspired by Italian Renaissance gardens, with classical and symmetrical proportions and architectural features. Amid the plantings are cherub statues and elegant stone steps leading to a pool (once the family swimming pool) surrounded by potted hydrangeas and asparagus vines. In this tranquil spot you can enjoy the appealing sounds of water from jets spouting into the pool.

For all of its bucolic charms, Winterthur is a well-organized site, offering guided tours and lectures; a thirty-minute tram ride (narrated by a guide); two unusually nice museum and gift shops; a restaurant and picnic areas; a library stocked with books on antiques, art, and history; and other amenities. For those who like to wander about on their own, a map and descriptive brochure are available at the visitor center.

❀ **Admission:** Fee.

Garden open: The museum and gardens are open Tuesday through Sunday 10:00 A.M. to 5:00 P.M.; closed New Year's Day, Thanksgiving, and Christmas. The library is open Monday through Friday 8:30 A.M. to 4:30 P.M.

Further information: General admission includes a tour of the museum galleries (on your own) and a stroll or tram ride in the gardens. Reservations are required only for special tours on decorative arts and gardens.
Directions: Winterthur is 30 miles southwest of Philadelphia. Take Route 1 west to Hamorton (just before Longwood Gardens), then go south on Route 52 to Winterthur.

Don't Miss ...

4. The George Read II House and Garden

42 The Strand, **New Castle**, DE; (302) 322–8411;
www.hsd.org/read.htm

THIS IS A HISTORIC HOUSE and garden in a wonderful town for a visit. Currently being restored to its 1847–48 style (following the precepts of Andrew Jackson Downing), the Read gardens feature both formal flower beds outlined with boxwood and a fine landscape of specimen shrubs and trees.

✿ **Admission:** Fee.

Garden open: Tuesday through Saturday 10:00 A.M. to 4:00 P.M., Sunday noon to 4:00 P.M., from March 1 to December 31; open weekends only in January and February; closed on holidays. Tours available by advance registration.

5. Hagley Museum and Library

Route 141, **Wilmington,** DE; (302) 658–2400; www.hagley.lib.de.us

THIS 320-ACRE SITE of the first du Pont powder works gives visitors an amazing glimpse into early-nineteenth-century industrial and community life through some sixty buildings, as well as justly famous gardens. These elegant, restored flower and vegetable gardens feature French-style flower beds in geometric patterns; borders of dwarf, espaliered fruit trees; a kitchen garden; an intriguing Italianate garden built upon some ruins; and a variety of woodsy trails best visited in spring, when azaleas, dogwoods, and rhododendrons are at their best.

✿ **Admission:** Free.

Garden open: Daily 9:30 A.M. to 4:30 P.M.

Gardenwalks in Maryland

[Carpet beds are like] the lace, linen, and ribbon decorations of a lady's dress—being essential ornaments, and yet to be introduced sparingly. . . . Beware of frequently breaking open stretches of lawn for them. Imagine bits of lace or bows of ribbon stuck promiscuously over the body and skirt of a lady's dress.

—FRANK J. SCOTT, 1870

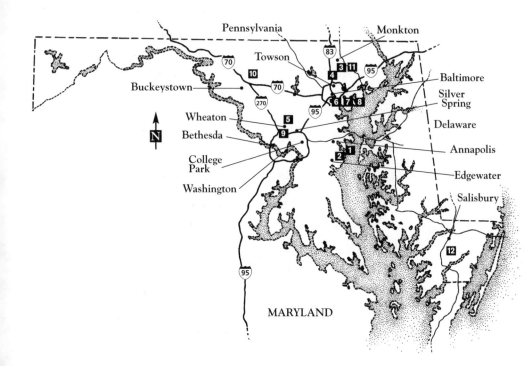

1. Annapolis: William Paca
   Garden
2. Edgewater: London Town House
   and Garden
3. Monkton: Ladew Topiary
   Gardens
4. Towson: Hampton National
   Historic Site
5. Wheaton: Brookside Gardens

Don't Miss . . .

6. Baltimore: Cylburn Garden
   Center
7. Baltimore: Druid Hill Park
   Conservatory
8. Baltimore: Sherwood Gardens
9. Bethesda: McCrillis Gardens
10. Buckeystown: Lilypons Water
    Gardens
11. Monkton: Breezewood
12. Salisbury: Salisbury State
    University Arboretum

1. William Paca Garden

186 Prince George Street, **Annapolis**, MD; (410) 263–5553;
www.annapolis.org

*T*HE ORDERLY CHARM of the colonial garden must have been particularly noticeable in the days when America was mostly wilderness. Yet when you visit a historic town such as Annapolis, you realize that an elegant and imaginative town garden like that behind the William Paca House was one of many similar pleasure gardens on streets of fine homes. Jefferson is said to have commented that Annapolis's "gardens are better than those of Williamsburg." Unfortunately few are now left, and we are all the more grateful for the careful restoration and upkeep that make the Paca garden well worth a visit.

This walled garden is surprisingly large (two acres), considering its center-of-town location. The entire garden is made up of a series of five terraces. Boxwood hedges and brick paths divide one section from another, and the various levels are reached by small sets of steps. Two diagonal pathways intersect the more traditional squares of plantings, each one of which is laid out in a geometric pattern. There are several unusually charming outbuildings, Chinese latticework, a fish-shaped pond, an informal "wilderness area," and a profusion of carefully arranged plantings.

The Georgian mansion that William Paca built from 1763 to 1765 sits proudly on an Annapolis city street. Paca, a rich and prominent lawyer, was a signer of the Declaration of Independence, a senator, and a governor of Maryland. He had the house and garden designed in English Georgian five-part style. (The house is open to visitors interested in the finest colonial decor and antiques.)

After Paca left Annapolis in 1780, the estate was sold or leased many times during the next 180 years. Apparently something of a white elephant, the house was used by tenants as a doctor's office and a boardinghouse; in 1901 it became a hotel. The garden similarly had a long and uncertain history: At various times parts of it became a parking lot, a gas station, and a bus station.

The house was altered extensively by the hotel owners. The original structure became the lobby for the 200-room hotel, and neo-Georgian columns were added to the front of the building. A large part of the gardens became a parking lot for the hotel's bustling business. Carvel Hall, as the old Paca estate was known, became a center of Annapolis's political and social life.

But in 1965 the hotel owners decided to sell the property to real estate developers for an office and apartment complex. Like so much of our country's past, the Paca house was soon to disappear. (The gardens had already virtually vanished.) The Historic Annapolis Foundation came to the rescue and for $275,000 bought the house, while the state paid for the restoration of most of the original garden.

The ensuing restoration took historians and archeologists years to complete. Using archival drawings and texts, scraps of extant original material, information unearthed during excavations, and even a portrait of Paca standing in front of his garden, experts reconstructed both the house and garden in its eighteenth-century elegance. The original garden wall (stretching for more than a third of a mile) was still partly standing; the rest was reconstructed. This is truly a success story, for the original estate was well worth recreating.

Your garden walk will begin at the back door of the Paca house. On your left is the rose garden, including nine types of roses grown in Paca's time. Directly across from it you'll find a geometrically arranged seasonal flower bed. Farther to the right is a traditional physic garden of medicinal plants. On the outer edges of both sides of the garden are "necessaries"—quaint privies now used for storing tools. Herbs, vegetables, and a fruit garden are next as you move away from the house. Traditional eighteenth-century methods are used for pruning. Particularly nice in winter is the holly parterre, to the immediate right of the central pathway and down the first set of steps. Opposite is the formal topiary garden. Plantings in all of these gardens include both native Maryland specimens and rare and unusual plants grown and maintained in the eighteenth-century manner.

Down the next set of stairs you'll find the canal and a Chinese-style bridge leading to the pond (shaped like a giant fish), and the summerhouse. In Paca's time the water aspects of the garden were both practical and pretty. Springhouse, canals, pond, and underground passages provided water for house and garden and even a cold bathhouse. Excavations unearthed the original brick foundations for the architectural elements of the gardens, including the summerhouse, the pavilion, and the bridge. Charles Willson Peale's portrait of Paca shows the picturesque domed summerhouse; it was reconstructed accordingly. The Chinese latticework bridge (lattice as a design element is also found within the house) was popular in eighteenth-century English design books, and here it adds to the graceful charm of trellises and gateways throughout the garden.

At the very rear of the garden, you'll find the cold bathhouse (no doubt a pleasant addition in the hot Maryland summer) and the springhouse; archeologists found the original conduits for the spring, as well as a basin and floorboards.

The Paca gardens are both practical and aesthetically pleasing —a combination that the best colonial gardens seem to have created effortlessly. It is always hard to believe that despite the dramatic and unsettled times they lived in, early settlers in the colonies cared so much for beauty and design.

❄ **Admission:** Fee.

Garden open: Monday through Saturday 10:00 A.M. to 4:00 P.M., Sunday noon to 4:00 P.M. from March through December; in the winter only on Friday, Saturday, and Sunday. Closed on major holidays.

Further information: You may visit the gardens without visiting the house.

Directions: Take Route 50/301 to Route 70 into Annapolis. Follow signs to the historic district. From the State House in the center of the city, take Maryland Avenue, which intersects Prince George Street. The Paca House is on Prince George Street between Maryland Avenue and East Street.

2. London Town House and Garden

839 Londontown Road, **Edgewater,** MD; (410) 222–1919; www.historiclondontown.com

*L*ONDON TOWN is a sturdy brick Georgian house (circa 1760) once called the Publik House. In the colonial days when London Town (not far from Annapolis) was a tobacco exporting center, the house was a ferry boatman's house and colonial meeting spot, and then it was used for years as an inn and finally as an almshouse. It sits serenely on a bluff overlooking Maryland's South River and a small creek and a stream—almost surrounded, in fact, by water. Its view is pretty (despite modern housing just across one vista), and its woodland garden grounds are unusually naturalistic for a colonial-era site. In fact, a public building of this sort would probably not have had a pleasure garden at all, so a naturalistic woodland was planned at the site's restoration not long ago. Currently a fashionable spot for weddings, London Town is now a National Historic Landmark with an eight-acre garden.

These eight acres are on a hillside that runs down to the water's edge—and all along the curving route to the river (with staircases here and there) are various plantings and benches for enjoying the woodland gardens and the vista beyond. Described as a series of gardens within a garden, the planting areas are linked by a pathway. A self-guiding map is available; it takes you from the Berms (where narcissus, peonies, and perennials are planted near the house) to the Spring Walk (featuring a 30-foot climbing hydrangea), Azalea Walk, a charming gazebo with a panoramic view, a winter garden with a viburnum walkway, a Camellia Walk, and on through holly and wildflowers. Eventually you find yourself at the Dell Pond near the river's edge, where aquatic plants flourish. This is not a long walk, but it is hilly and somewhat rustic.

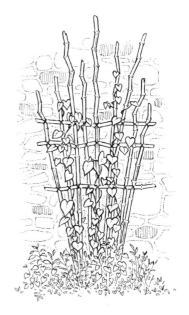

Of added interest are the archeological digs on-site. Among the many recent finds are a series of foundations and thousands of well-preserved artifacts from what was once Scorton, the eighteenth-century home of Dr. Richard Hill. A surgeon, ship owner, and plantation owner, Hill was also a naturalist who may have met John Bartram in 1737 (see the write-up of the Bartram garden in Philadelphia). More than 1,000 items have been found in digs at this site; some are on view here.

❀ **Admission:** Fee.

Garden open: The house and grounds are open Tuesday through Saturday 10:00 A.M. to 4:00 P.M., and noon to 4:00 P.M. Sunday from April to November; open in the winter by appointment. We recommend visiting in spring.

Further information: Tours and educational programs available.

Directions: From Route 50/301, which is the route to Annapolis from the Washington area, take Route 665 (exit 22). Take Route 2 south, go over the South River Bridge and continue ⁶⁄₁₀ mile to the light at Mayo Road (Route 253). Make a left turn and follow ⁸⁄₁₀ mile to the light at Londontown Road. Turn left and go 1 mile to the end.

3. Ladew Topiary Gardens

3535 Jarrettsville Pike, **Monkton**, MD; (410) 557-9570;
www.ladewgardens.com

A FOXHUNT WITHIN THE GROUNDS of a formal garden? As
unlikely as it may sound, you will indeed find one at Ladew
Topiary Gardens in Monkton, Maryland. But instead of a lively
scene of red-coated riders and yelping hounds, you'll find a quiet,
green sanctuary. Fortunately for the potential victim, no real foxhunt takes place here—only a giant topiary version of one.

Ladew Gardens were the creation of Harvey Smith Ladew, a
prominent and somewhat eccentric New York socialite; he moved
to the Maryland countryside to pursue his equally great passions for
foxhunting and building gardens. Some years after his death, the
fifteen gardens on this twenty-two-acre site were restored to their
former splendor. Filled with surprises at every turn, they reflect
Ladew's wit, whimsy, and peculiar interests.

One of the most delightful spots is, unquestionably, the plant-
sculpture foxhunt tableau, which includes two horses and riders
jumping over a fence to follow six clipped-yew hounds in hot pur-
suit of a fox. Grassy walks throughout these green acres take you to
other topiary delights found among hedges, behind fountains, and
around walkways: a flock of twelve graceful swans "floating" atop a
hedge; seahorses; a lyrebird; a Scottie running toward his bowl and
ball; and the somewhat incongruous forms of Winston Churchill's
victory sign, a Chinese junk, and a large Buddha.

More conventional gardens representing a variety of styles also
grace the elegant premises. Among them are a carefully tended wild
garden (not such a contradiction of terms within this context); an
old-fashioned Victorian flower garden; a rose garden enclosed in a
circular brick wall; a yellow garden; a white garden; a water lily
garden; and even a Garden of Eden, with a statue of Adam and Eve
surrounded by azaleas and . . . apple trees. A terrace garden features

steps flanked by austere-looking topiary obelisks in formal rows. A Temple of Venus (Ladew's "folly," perhaps) overlooks the entire scene from a lofty perch.

The Ladew Gardens are both formal and romantic in tone. Their combination of charm, surprise, and beauty will appeal to young and old alike. (Children will delight in finding and identifying the topiary forms.) The estate also includes an elegant home filled with travel memorabilia, artifacts, and photographs reflecting Ladew's active social life and travels.

✤ **Admission:** Fee.
Garden open: Daily from April to the end of October.
Further information: You can wander around on your own in the garden, but you need to sign up for a tour to visit the house.
Directions: From Baltimore take Route 83 to Interstate 695; take exit 27B (Route 146). Cross over the bridge and bear left onto Route 146, the Jarrettsville Pike. Travel 14 miles to Ladew Gardens.

4. Hampton National Historic Site

535 Hampton Lane, **Towson,** MD; (410) 828–9480;
www.nps.gov/hamp

*T*HERE IS SOMETHING unusually evocative and romantic about this house and garden; it will also be of great interest to garden historians. The elegant mansion, Hampton Hall (1783–90), is large and particularly pretty, with its warm, peach-toned exterior and felicitous design with delicate cupola on top. It is set in a rolling green landscape that has the feel of rural Maryland, although it is just beyond the highway. The vast agricultural and industrial plantation, owned by Charles Carnan Ridgely and his descendants until 1948, once comprised 24,000 acres including tobacco farms, and an iron mine and foundry. Most of it is gone now, of course, but what remains (sixty-seven acres) is gracious and thoroughly surprising. Among the many reminders of the past glory of Hampton are the stables, the lovely (reconstructed) orangerie, the smokehouse, and the small family cemetery.

The entire estate combines eighteenth- and nineteenth-century designs in a fascinating way. At first, as you walk around the grounds and behind the house, you see vast lawns and dozens of very old trees. There are numerous notable trees; to the credit of the National Park Service, many of these still stand 200 years after planting—evoking bygone days in a way that no historically dressed tour guides could do. The layout of the landscape followed the ideas of Andrew Jackson Downing, the preeminent garden designer of the mid-nineteenth century. Among these great leaning, bending trees are gnarled catalpas (among the most romantic), copper beeches, Norway spruce, a 115-foot-high pecan tree, tulip trees, and the largest cedar of Lebanon we've ever seen (it is believed that the seedling was carted in a shoe box from the Middle East!). The serpentine path takes you among the trees, through the wisteria arbors, past a series of artistically placed ancient marble vases, and all the way to the end of this Victorian-style garden.

But is it the end? When you arrive at the path's termination, you suddenly find you are at the top of a hill. Below you lies the crowning glory of Hampton Hall: the parterre formal gardens. Down grassy ramps—the American eighteenth-century version of England's more proper staircases—are formal gardens in four neatly arranged, terraced rectangles. The gardens were installed from 1790 to 1801 and are both surprising and—seen as they are from a distance above—thoroughly decorative. These parterre gardens are among the largest such terraced gardens in Maryland. The original idea of the grassy hillside terraces was an optical fantasy, because when viewed from the cupola of the house on the hill, they seem quite flat! The owner had every intention of bringing European-style elegance to Hampton Hall.

Each parterre is different, though all are outlined in boxwood. One features peonies, another roses, a third spring bulbs. Each is laid out in thoroughly geometric style, with its patterns accented by paths of white pebbles and rows of charming round boxwood plantings. Seen from above, these gardens are a treat to behold.

A visit here can of course include a tour of the mansion as well as the gardens—or you can pick up a very good flyer and walk around the grounds by yourself. Hampton neatly illustrates the changing ideas about gardens through American history; it also is one of the prettiest garden landscapes in Maryland and a delightful place for a picnic.

❀ **Admission:** Free.

Garden open: Daily 9:00 A.M. to 5:00 P.M.

Further information: Tours are offered from 9:00 A.M. to 4:00 P.M.

Directions: From the Baltimore Beltway (I–695) north of Baltimore, take exit 27B and make an immediate hard right turn at the end of the ramp onto Hampton Lane. Follow signs.

5. Brookside Gardens

1500 Glenallan Avenue, **Wheaton,** MD; (301) 962–1400; www.mc-mncppc.org/parks/brookside

*J*UST NORTH OF WASHINGTON, D.C., in the rolling hills and busy, built-up suburbs of Maryland, you'll find the particularly pleasant landscape known as Brookside Gardens. This extensive fifty-acre garden lends itself to long walks, good conversation, and all-season recreation. There are both indoor conservatories and formal and informal gardens, a series of ponds with Japanese gardens and teahouse, and wonderful stands of trees.

A relatively recent addition to the green spaces of the Mid-Atlantic states, Brookside was planned in the 1960s, planted in the 1970s, and is still evolving today. All kinds of programs for educational and recreational use take place at Brookside, but the designers have wisely left much of the area free of the overplanning, broken-up spaces, signage, and other intrusions that bedevil so many modern garden parks.

The conservatory is a charming, not very large glasshouse with permanent tropical displays and five seasonal sections that can be seen at any time of year. Brookside is a particularly good place to visit in the winter, because you have a choice of indoor and outdoor gardens (there is, in fact, a "winter garden").

Outdoors you'll find gently hilly acreage, with garden areas distributed throughout. You can walk on paths or across the hills themselves. Nearest to the conservatory are formal gardens, including a perennial garden of bulbs and mums (in bloom spring through fall), a yew garden, a rock garden, a rose garden graced by a pergola, an educational and thematic garden, a round garden that features plum trees, a fragrance garden with a fountain, and even a gazebo.

More informal areas include a butterfly garden, an aquatic garden that is delightful to behold, a viburnum garden that includes forty varieties, and a specialty in spring: the rhododendron and azalea garden with some 400 varieties planted across seven acres of the landscape.

Of particular note is the Japanese-style Gude garden. This nine-acre area—at the farthest edge of the park—has sculpted ponds and elegant trees along with a charming bridge and teahouse.

Brookside sits within the large Wheaton Regional Park, and you can combine your garden visit with bicycling, horseback riding, ice-skating, tennis, and other recreational activities. It is a true oasis in an area filled with bustle, and we recommend it for a family walk.

Admission: Free.

Garden open: Daily.

Directions: From Interstate 495 (the Capital Beltway) north of Washington, D.C., take the Georgia Avenue exit north for 3 ¹/₁₀ miles. Go right on Randolph Road for 2 blocks, then right onto Glenallan Avenue to the entrance to Brookside on your right.

Don't Miss . . .

6. Cylburn Garden Center

4915 Green Spring Avenue, **Baltimore,** MD; (410) 367–2217; www.cylburnassociation.org

AMID 176 ACRES belonging to the Maryland Ornithological Society is a Victorian mansion surrounded by a greenhouse, formal gardens, and display gardens. Birders will be pleased to know there are wildflower trails through a bird sanctuary—a good vantage point for viewing birds.

Admission: Free.

Garden open: Daily dawn to dusk.

7. Druid Hill Park Conservatory

McCulloch Street and Gwynns Falls Parkway, **Baltimore,** MD; (410) 396–0180

THIS RECENTLY RESTORED century-old conservatory is filled with tropical plants. Watch for special seasonal exhibits, especially at Christmastime. Outside you can walk through a small, one-acre display garden filled with spring, summer, and fall blossoms.

Admission: Free.

Garden open: Daily 10:00 A.M. to 4:00 P.M.

8. Sherwood Gardens

Stratford Road, **Baltimore**, MD; (410) 366–2572

THIS IS A SEVEN-ACRE community-operated garden in a particularly pretty section of Baltimore, where the elegant mansions all seem to have pretty gardens too. The city block called Sherwood Gardens is noted for its tulips, so visit (if you are in the vicinity) in tulip time, late April into May. The site was once a lake that had dried; in 1927 it became a public garden after the property was purchased and converted by a businessman named John Sherwood. Some 80,000 tulips bloom here, rather surprisingly in single color groups, often in asymmetrical flower beds. There are purple beds, pink beds, red beds—each filled with hundreds of waving tulips. The rest of the fairly flat landscape is grassy with occasional pretty flowering shrubs and trees—dogwoods, magnolias, and especially azaleas. This is primarily a local garden: Community organizations have adopt-a-bed areas, and there is even an annual tulip bulb dig. (We assume they keep the 80,000 bulb count constant, however!)

❀ **Admission:** Free.

Garden open: Year-round, but best visited from mid-April through mid-May for tulip and azalea time.

9. McCrillis Gardens

6910 Greentree Road, **Bethesda**, MD; (301) 365–5728;
www.montgomeryparksfnd.org

THIS GARDEN IS UNUSUAL in that its informally landscaped five acres are designed for shade. The plantings include some 750 varieties of azaleas, many from Japan. Visit in spring, although the garden is open year-round.

❀ **Admission:** Free.

Garden open: Year-round.

10. Lilypons Water Gardens

6800 Lilypons Road, **Buckeystown,** MD;
(301) 874-5133, (800) 723-7667;
www.lilypons.com

WATER GARDENING is becoming quite popular, and one of the old-est and largest water gardens in the nation provides both display gardens and all the necessaries to start your own. Set in a flat, strange network filling 300 acres, Lilypons (yes, named for the great operatic star) is composed of a series of rectangular aquatic gardens. In each pond are either varieties of water lilies and other water plants or types of fish that are happy in water gardens. The ambience is one of serious purpose, with workers in hip boots scooping specimens from the ponds, and visitors walking gingerly along the clayey raised pathways between aquatic wonders. A trip here is not necessarily the aesthetic experience you may expect from a garden visit, but it is interesting nonetheless, and you can watch small component parts of the garden being fished out and sold. Lilypons is a commercial (and mail-order) establishment.

✿ **Admission:** Free.
Garden open: Daily 9:30 A.M. to 5:30 P.M. from March through October; closed major holidays. We recommend visiting after May 1.

11. Breezewood

Hess Road, **Monkton,** MD; (301) 472-9438

THIS IS AN ASIAN ROCK GARDEN with an emphasis on Siamese culture. You'll find pagodas, a pool, and a museum of Buddhist culture and Southeast Asian art.

✿ **Admission:** Free.
Garden open: The first Sunday of each month, 2:00 to 6:00 P.M., from May through October.

12. Salisbury State University Arboretum

1101 Camden Avenue, **Salisbury,** MD; (410) 543–6000;
www.salisbury.edu/arboretum

Salisbury State University Arboretum in Maryland's Eastern Shore is a green oasis of beautiful specimen trees, carefully tended lawns, shrubs, and flower beds. The university, set in quiet, suburban surroundings, has in the past several years developed not only into a fully accredited (and still expanding) arboretum but also as a sculpture park surrounded by brick walkways, clipped hedges, courtyards, and fountains. Unlike most campuses, the grounds here are in part maintained by botany and horticulture students. You'll see a wonderful collection of magnolias—some impressively tall—giant hollies, ginkgoes, oaks, maples, and pines—some quite rare. A central focus is the gracious white-columned, airy pergola, complete with twenty-six different kinds of vines, hanging baskets, and potted plants.

With a copy of the well-designed and informative arboretum map (available at the Guerrieri University Center), you will discover a butterfly garden; a "secret" courtyard with low, graceful hedges surrounding brightly colored annuals and a central fountain; two greenhouses with tropical plants; a Japanese-style raked garden (under construction); and luxuriant carpets of creeping junipers and serpentine dwarf boxwoods. You can wander about these landscaped acres on your own or by guided tour (check at the Guerrieri Center for tour details).

❀ **Admission:** Free.
Garden open: Daily.

Gardenwalks in New Jersey

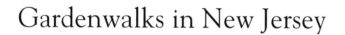*T*is in the Quiet Enjoyment of Rural Delights, the refreshing and Odoriferous Breezes of Garden Air, that That Deluge of Vapours and those Terrors of Hypocondraism, which croud and oppress the Head, are dispell'd. . . .

—STEPHEN SWITZER, 1718

New York

Ringwood

Saddle River

Morristown

Gladstone

Far Hills

Bernardsville

Somerville

New
Brunswick

Somerset

Lincroft

Middletown

Princeton

Pennsylvania

Lakewood

Trenton

Hamilton
Township

NEW JERSEY

Atlantic Ocean

Swainton

1. Bernardsville: Cross Estate
   Gardens
2. Far Hills: Leonard J. Buck
   Garden
3. Hamilton Township: Sayen
   Gardens
4. Lakewood: Georgian Court
   College
5. Middletown: Deep Cut Park
   Horticultural Center
6. Morristown: Frelinghuysen
   Arboretum
7. New Brunswick: Rutgers
   Gardens
8. Ringwood: Ringwood Manor
9. Ringwood: Skylands Botanical
   Garden

10. Somerset: Colonial Park
11. Somerville: Doris Duke
    Gardens

Don't Miss . . .

12. Gladstone: Willowwood
    Arboretum
13. Hamilton Township: Grounds
    for Sculpture
14. Lincroft: Lambertus C. Bobbink
    Memorial Rose Garden
15. Princeton: Prospect Garden
16. Saddle River: Waterford
    Gardens
17. Swainton: Leaming's Run
    Gardens

1. Cross Estate Gardens

Old Jockey Hollow Road, **Bernardsville,** NJ; (973) 543–4030;
www.crossestategardens.org

*T*HIS EXQUISITE SITE is neither large nor especially grand, but
its intimate walled gardens are among the loveliest we have
seen. Set in a historic area near Morristown National Historic Park
(of Revolutionary War fame), the gardens are part of an elegant
estate that was built as a summer retreat in 1905.

The site was laid out by a noted landscape designer named
Clarence Fowler, but it was apparently Julia Newbold Cross who was
the guiding inspiration for the English-style gardens. Cross, who
with her husband purchased the house in 1929, was a noted gardener, a member of the Royal Horticultural Society, and a longtime
president of the New York Horticultural Society. Now maintained
by dedicated volunteers (you might find them working there when
you visit, as we did), the gardens have been returned to their original glory after a long period of neglect.

The walled gardens are the centerpiece of a charming landscape that includes a vine-covered pergola, a mountain laurel allée,
and a shade garden planted with ferns, shrubs, and perennials. The
formal gardens are enclosed by walls and divided by geometric brick
paths. The plantings within the garden walls are delightful and ever
changing. As in a true English garden, there is a profusion of color
and texture and size, with flowers set in ornamental beds edged by
repeated plantings and ornamented by enchanting old-fashioned
urns and brickwork. Among the plantings you might see when you
visit are edgings of white-flowered periwinkle, English ivy, and boxwood surrounding lemon balm, butter bush, coralbells, potentilla,
lamb's ears, and numerous types of daylilies.

This is the kind of garden where you may truly hear birds sing or detect the sounds of a watercolorist swishing his brush in a glass (we saw several blissful painters during our visit).

✿ **Admission:** Free.

Garden open: Daily dawn to dusk.

Further information: The best season to visit is spring.

Directions: From New York, take Interstate 80 to Interstate 287 south. Turn at Harter Road (exit A—left) to Route 202 southbound. Turn off Route 202 (also called Mount Kemble Avenue) after ⁹⁄₁₀ mile; turn right at the traffic light onto Tempe Wick Road and continue 2 miles. Pass the entrance to Jockey Hollow, go left onto Leddell Road at waterfall and continue 1 ¹⁄₁₀ miles. Turn left onto a long driveway at the sign NEW JERSEY BRIGADE AREA—CROSS ESTATE GARDENS.

2. Leonard J. Buck Garden

11 Layton Road, **Far Hills**, NJ; (908) 234-2677;
www.park.co.somerset.nj.us/activities/gardens/gardens_Buck

*S*ET AMID some of New Jersey's prettiest rolling countryside of sprawling farms and thick stone walls is a naturalistic garden that looks as though it has been untouched by human hands.

A vast and inviting site deep within a rocky, narrow gorge surrounded by glacial ponds and massive rocky outcroppings, the Leonard J. Buck Garden is a delight to explore. Although it may appear at first to be a wilderness, it is in fact a carefully nurtured environment.

This thirty-three-acre garden, now one of the premier rock gardens in the country, was designed in the 1930s with great care by Leonard J. Buck, a wealthy mining engineer. Fascinated by the giant volcanic rock outcroppings on his property, Buck worked with a landscape architect, Zenon Schreiber, to develop a naturalistic garden using these extraordinary geological formations as the basis for his design. As one of the early ecologists, Buck was interested in the symbiotic relationship between rocks, soil, and plants. His aim was to make his garden look as though it had been created by nature.

Buck and Schreiber set about their task like archaeologists and artists. They unearthed rock formations that had been buried beneath loose traprock and reshaped and sculpted them to add to their visual appeal. Around each outcropping they carefully placed plantings suitable to its particular microclimate and exposure. Always a lover of exotic plants, Buck filled his valley with some rare examples as well as more familiar varieties. He laid out connecting pathways where wildflowers have since proliferated. He even built a dam.

His imagination and vision, along with the landscape's natural beauty and its continuing evolution, have made this a place of enchantment. Rhododendrons, azaleas, ferns, heaths, and heathers grace wooded paths and meadows; ponds and waterfalls add a touch of romance. But the rocky outcroppings with their individual gardens are what make this garden special.

Each of the thirteen massive formations has a name (not always labeled, however), such as Big Rock, shaped like a dinosaur, or Horseshoe Rock, so shaped by an ancient waterfall. As you wind your way around the surrounding paths, you'll notice that each rock garden is distinctive from the next. Among the many varieties of plants you might see (depending on the season) are wild columbines, clematis, viburnum, stonecrop, white violets, succulents, mosses, blueberries, ferns, lady's slippers, and wild orchids.

If you're adventuresome and quite fit (note that the terrain is fairly hilly) and have a particular interest in alpine rock gardens, you won't want to miss this rare place. And if you're not bothered by the occasional noisy intrusion of a nearby highway, you will think you're walking through a remote wilderness.

You can take a guided tour if you are so inclined. However, this is a garden to savor at your own pace, and detailed walking guides and lists of plants in bloom or in fruit are available at the entrance. (The garden is operated by the Somerset County Park Commission, which regularly publishes informative material of geological and botanic interest.) Whether your garden pleasure is scientific or purely aesthetic, we have no hesitation in suggesting you put on your sturdy walking shoes, gather together flyers and plant listings, and head for the New Jersey hills' best rock garden.

❀ **Admission:** Donation requested.
Garden open: Monday through Saturday 10:00 A.M. to 4:00 P.M., Sunday noon to 4:00 P.M. (winter) or noon to 5:00 P.M. (summer).
Further information: Guided tours are available.
Directions: From I–287 north take exit 22. From I–287 south take exit 22B. Follow Route 202 north to Far Hills. At train station turn right just before the tracks onto Liberty Corner/Far Hills Road; go about 1 mile and turn right at Layton Road. The garden is on the left.

3. Sayen Gardens

155 Hughes Drive, **Hamilton Township,** NJ; (609) 890–3874; www.sayengardens.org

*J*T IS ALWAYS INTRIGUING to observe an artistic work in progress, whether it be a painting, a sculpture, or a garden. You note the existing colors, textures, shapes, and general design and wonder what the final outcome will be. Sayen Gardens in semirural New Jersey, just east of Trenton, is a garden in progress. Although much of it is now in place, additional parts of this thirty-acre site are being developed.

The property was once the country estate of Frederick Sayen, a rubber industrialist whose passion was botany. From his worldwide travels he brought back many plants, exotic and otherwise, including unusual varieties of azaleas and rhododendrons. He began planning and creating gardens around his English-style mansion, which were not completed during his lifetime. In 1985 Hamilton Township bought the property from the Sayen family and opened it to the public in 1988.

Garden designers have since been following a ten-year plan that more or less corresponds to Frederick Sayen's original idea for the gardens. The once completely flat landscape was contoured (for better drainage), becoming a site of gentle hills. Existing overgrown beds and trails had to be reclaimed, and new ones were formed.

From the moment you arrive, you are aware that Sayen Gardens is a relatively new site. A pristine brick walk bordered by profuse impatiens marks the graceful entrance. You then reach a striking contemporary-style garden situated on an artificially created mound in front of the mansion. Its enormous, carefully—but not formally—placed boulders (excavated when the landscape was contoured) make it too dramatic to be called a rock garden. You can view it as you meander on a rustic woodchip path up and around groupings of eclectic plantings. The combination of exotic grasses and unusual plants alongside more traditional varieties is attractive and modern. The overall arrangement is also spectacular in terms of colors, shapes, and textures. Unlike traditional botanic gardens, nothing is labeled at Sayen; to identify these eye-catching varieties, you must consult one of the gardeners on staff.

A number of paths through pine woods laced with wildflowers lead to other gardens, including some under construction. (Be prepared for muddy spots.) One trail takes you to a pretty Japanese-style garden, where you'll see a pond with traditional arched bridge and gazebo surrounded by tall, willowy grasses. If you visit in springtime, you can enjoy a spectacle of—we are told—80,000 dazzling daffodils in April and masses of azaleas and rhododendrons in brilliant profusion in May.

Among the gardens in the planning stage is a fairly large rose garden. And there is talk of restoring the Sayen house to an earlier period. At Sayen Gardens you can see gardens in the making, and if you are planning your own garden and need some ideas, you will surely find inspiration here.

✿ **Admission:** Free.

Garden open: Daily during daylight hours.

Directions: From the New Jersey Turnpike, take exit 7 to Route 33 west. Turn left on Whitehorse Road to the stop sign. Turn right onto Nottingham Way and left at Hamilton Square onto Mercer Street for 3 blocks. Turn left onto Hughes Drive. The entrance to the gardens is on your left.

4. Georgian Court College

900 Lakewood Avenue, **Lakewood,** N J; (732) 364–2200; www.georgian.edu

*T*HE VERY NAME "Georgian Court" suggests an eighteenth-century setting in an English countryside, with a stately home, arched bridges over gently flowing water, white marble statues, and formal gardens. We were astonished and delighted to find exactly such a place hidden away in Ocean County, New Jersey, a treasure for garden explorers and art lovers as well as for more than 1,000 college students.

Georgian Court College is a beautifully situated campus that was once a large private estate. It is enclosed by walls along a wide shady street. When you enter its palatial gates, you come directly upon a setting of such felicitous proportions and so many neoclassical sculptures that you find it hard to equate it with the general run of American college campuses. Instead of modern kinetic sculpture, you find a fountain statue of Apollo; instead of hard trodden paths from dorm to dorm, you find stone walkways through formal sunken flower beds and a Japanese teahouse.

The college (and undergraduate Catholic women's institution, with coed night and graduate divisions) was once the home of George Jay Gould, the financier and railroad magnate. Its 175 acres were purchased in 1896. Gould hired a noted architect, Bruce Price, to design the home in the outskirts of the winter resort of Lakewood. The mansion itself (now a college building) was constructed of gray stucco with white terra-cotta brick, marble, and wood. The interior of the original building is elegantly paneled and maintained. There is an indoor marble pool; outdoors, where the grounds were designed to match the Georgian-era architecture, there is a lagoon and a sunken garden and a magnificent promenade.

Gould's son, Kingdon Gould, sold the estate to the Sisters of Mercy in 1924, and though they transformed it into an educational institution, happily they left its distinctive character intact. In 1985 Georgian Court College was declared a National Historic Landmark.

The estate is situated along the banks of a good-size lake called Lake Carasaljo in the pines area of south-central New Jersey. As you enter the gates, you will come first to the Italian or classical garden, which harmonizes so nicely with the architecture of the original mansion. This elliptical formal garden consists of sixteen flower beds bordered by boxwood. The flower beds are meticulously maintained. A Japanese garden, made in 1925, includes a teahouse, wooden bridges, and shrubbery.

As you leave the flower gardens and walk into the center of the campus, you will find the rolling green lawns crossed by pathways and dotted with classical marble sculptures. The most notable sculpture is the Apollo Fountain designed by John Massey Rhind, a sculptor of public monuments and statues. Its horses plunge dramatically from the serene water, its white marble Apollo heroically in command.

A flight of wide marble steps takes you down to the lake edge and connects the original sunken garden and a lagoon. A promenade in the opposite direction (leading to classroom and library buildings) is flanked on either side by classical sculptures.

❀ **Admission:** Free.

Garden open: Daily dawn to dusk.

Further information: The campus is mostly flat and wheelchair accessible.

Directions: From the Garden State Parkway, take exit 91. Bear right after the toll plaza and proceed through the first intersection (Burnt Tavern Road) to the next traffic light, at County Line Road, which you take for approximately 5 miles to Route 9. Turn left onto Route 9 south and continue to Ninth Street. Turn right onto Ninth Street and proceed through the Forest Avenue intersection to Lakewood Avenue. The entrance to the college is to your right.

5. Deep Cut Park Horticultural Center

352 Red Hill Road, **Middletown,** N J; (732) 671–6050;
www.monmouthcountyparks.com/parks/deep_cut/deep_cut.asp

*W*HEN VISITING GARDENS you hardly expect to be involved in a mystery story. It comes as a surprise, then, to learn that Deep Cut Park Horticultural Center in rural Monmouth County is literally a garden with a shady past.

The site was farmland through the nineteenth century. In 1890 it was taken over by the sheriff for nonpayment of taxes. After a series of owners, it fell into the hands of the infamous Mafia boss Vito Genovese in 1935.

Genovese transformed the old farm and created several gardens. True to his reputation as a big spender, he had his Italian stonemasons build extensive walls—including the unusual festoon-like stone wall surrounding the property—and a series of ornamental pools, a huge swimming pool, and a replica of Mount Vesuvius, smoke effects and all! He imported rare plants and trees (among these are the gnarled weeping hemlocks still overlooking the terrace gardens).

In 1937, when Genovese was being investigated by the authorities, his family suddenly left for Europe. During their absence a mysterious fire destroyed the mansion—an incident that remains unsolved to this day. After World War II (Genovese had spent it in Italy, working with Mussolini), the mafioso was returned to the United States to stand trial for murder. Not surprisingly, the key witness against him was poisoned and the case dropped. In 1949 Genovese sold his property to Mary Gladys Cubbage, who eventually sold it to Karl and Marjorie Wihtol just a few years before Genovese was sent to jail on narcotics charges. The Wihtols built the existing house (now the visitor center) and greenhouses and created many of the gardens you see today. In 1977 the county park system took over the property, converting the house into classrooms, a library, a gift shop, and offices.

Notwithstanding its turbulent past, Deep Cut is a pleasant place to visit—and very peaceful. Named for the narrow stream that forms a deep cut in the landscape, it includes fifty-three acres of hillside gardens and greenhouses planned as a living plant catalog for the home gardener.

The gardens are arranged informally, with one flowing naturally into the next, surrounded by nice, hilly views. The first garden you come to, after parking your car, is the Butterfly and

Hummingbird Garden. Colorful annuals, perennials, and shrubs have been planted to attract these species. A nearby water lily pond is graced with a pretty fountain. Next you see formal beds decorated with plants in delicate shades of green and silver. Behind is the horticultural center. Here you can pick up a walking guide of the gardens.

Stroll down the path to the hillside gardens. On a summer day you will enjoy the Shade Garden with its canopy of dogwood, tulip, cedar, poplar, and cherry trees. Nearby is the Azalea and Rhododendron Walk; the Rockery (where Genovese's huge weeping hemlocks tower over three cascading pools); and a delightful orchard, filled with dwarf fruit and nut trees. If you continue on the walkways, you will come to a pretty wisteria-covered pergola, a pond, and a meadow. It was at this site that Genovese built his lavish pool, now buried. Instead of a pool you will see meadow wildflowers in late spring and summer.

The "working environment" sections of Deep Cut come next: a dried flower production field (where annuals and perennials are grown for use in craft classes); demonstration vegetable gardens in raised beds; and a composting site, complete with valuable information for the amateur gardener.

Don't miss the greenhouse, where you can enjoy displays of succulents, orchids, and houseplants. (The succulent collection was obtained by Marjorie Wihtol using the barter system.) Naturalists on staff are available for information concerning any of the plants you find here or throughout the gardens.

If you love roses you will want to visit in June or September to see those at Deep Cut, which have received prestigious awards. Early springtime brings forth clumps of daffodils, as well as blooming magnolias, dogwoods, and rhododendrons. May is tulip month, with thousands bursting forth in brilliant colors. Between classes, seminars, plant demonstrations, and displays, you will find plenty to do and see here at any time of year. You might wish to combine this visit with a walk in Tatum Park, directly across the street. This large nature preserve includes inviting trails and picnic tables.

✿ **Admission:** Free.

Garden open: Daily June to September, 8:00 A.M. to 8:00 P.M.; October to May, 8:00 A.M. to 4:30 P.M.

Further information: Operated by the Monmouth County Park Commission, the center offers a reference library, classrooms, and many programs concerning horticulture.

Directions: From the Garden State Parkway, take exit 114. Go east toward Middletown for 1½ miles to reach the center (on your right).

6. Frelinghuysen Arboretum

53 East Hanover Avenue, **Morristown,** NJ; (973) 326–7600;
www.parks.morris.nj.us/parks/frelarbmain

*T*HIS ESTATE consists of 127 acres divided into botanical garden units. It is a bustling place, filled with activity. As a regional center for horticultural programs, including many educational events, Frelinghuysen might not be described as a contemplative swatch of natural beauty. But there are nice forest and meadow paths, with shrubbery and trees well labeled for educational purposes; very pretty perennial flower beds; a shade garden; and a winter garden with hollies, snowdrops, and winter jasmine.

Among the most distinctive aspects of this busy place, however, are its gardens for the disabled and the blind: the Vera M. Scherer Garden for people with special needs, and the Pikaart Garden, a braille nature trail. Both are well designed and unusually successful.

The Scherer Garden is conceived as a tool to teach how gardens can be made more accessible. For example, raised flower beds eliminate bending or stretching and accommodate gardeners in wheelchairs. (The Frelinghuysen includes horticultural therapy programs among its many activities.) The Scherer Garden is worth a visit for its ingenious ideas about both accessibility and easy-care flower and herbs.

Described as a "scent, touch and feel garden," the Pikaart Garden is carefully labeled in braille. Gardeners have done a fine job of combining textured and fragrant plants. One interesting feature is a substitute pond—actually a bugleweed bed (blue in spring)—complete with brass crane statues and a bridge and stream. This fantasy pond is surrounded by plants that often grow at water's edge, such as Japanese or candelabra primrose and mountain laurel. Many textured plants include the dwarf horsetail, the heart-leaved begonia, and a variety of ferns.

❋ **Admission:** Free.
Garden open: Daily 8:00 A.M. to dusk except holidays.
Further information: Sections are wheelchair accessible.
Directions: From I–287, take exit 36A from the north and exit 36 from the south. Turn right at Ridgedale Avenue. Turn right at East Hanover Avenue. Entrance is ¼ mile on the right.

7. Rutgers Gardens

Ryder's Lane, **New Brunswick**, N J; (732) 932–8451;
www.aesop.rutgers.edu

*T*HERE ARE ALL KINDS of reasons to visit Rutgers Gardens, but we were particularly taken with its oddest feature: a bamboo forest. If you have ever seen ancient Asian art with its fearsome tigers creeping through a bamboo forest, you will no doubt recognize this mysterious and fascinating type of forest.

Here you'll see hundreds and hundreds of bamboo trees. They grow close together and stand tall and thin and straight against the sky, leaving a carpet of pale leaves beneath them. This is a sight to stay with you. A professor at the university planted only a few of these trees (he needed some bamboo poles), and then nature was allowed free rein. The result is breathtaking. We walked through the forest on a soft floor of creamy leaves, and around us the trees made a soaring pattern of vertical and occasionally tipping lines.

Rutgers Gardens are of course much more than bamboo groves. These are teaching and research gardens, specimen gardens, working gardens, community gardens. They are for students and scholars and garden enthusiasts who interest themselves in the many varieties of American holly trees (the most comprehensive collection in the country), in grafting different types of gloriously pink dogwood with one another, in how various plants grow in the shade and sun.

You can walk through twenty-five or thirty acres of these gardens and discover both beauty and plant lore. There are greenhouses where the minute work takes place. Outdoor paths take you to see all kinds of azaleas, an architect-designed evergreen garden, a series of stewartia trees with dappled bark from Japan and Korea, and even a brook with waterfalls that create an aquatic plant environment. There is a rare virgin forest, a large one and a blessing in this overbuilt area of New Jersey. And there are even thematic gardens whose themes are changed each year (fragrances, colors, and species are among recent choices).

We have found few such research gardens in the Mid-Atlantic, though they are common at the great land-grant colleges; Rutgers was established as one in 1921. (Another is Cornell University in Ithaca.) A visit here is a wonderful way to learn about gardens—and don't miss the walk through the bamboo.

❀ **Admission:** Fee.

Garden open: Daily 8:30 A.M. to dusk from May through September, and 8:30 A.M. to 4:30 P.M. from October through April.

Directions: From the New Jersey Turnpike, take exit 9 to Route 1 south (toward New Brunswick). Exit at Ryder's Lane (crossing under the highway to the opposite side of the road). Follow signs.

8. Ringwood Manor

Route 17, **Ringwood**, NJ; (973) 962–7031;
www.ringwoodmanor.com

*S*ET AMID the hilly terrain of the Ramapo Mountains is a most
unusual sculpture garden—partly rural retreat and partly European landscape design, with no less a garden than Versailles as its
model. Ringwood Manor is a large, imposing nineteenth-century
mansion surrounded by a magnificent sweep of green lawns, giant
trees, stone walls, formal gardens, orchards, lake, and forest. Designated a National Historic Landmark District, Ringwood is a place
to walk, picnic, and enjoy the art and ambience of another time.

Ringwood was a center of iron mining and munitions from
before the Revolutionary War until the end of World War I. The
site had major importance during the Revolution: The Continental
Army depended greatly upon Ringwood's iron production under
the ownership of Peter Hasenclever and his American Iron Company. In addition, Ringwood was home to Robert Erskine, whom
General Washington appointed as his army geographer. Erskine
produced some 300 maps for the Continental Army and is buried
at Ringwood. You'll see a charming old stone building or two from
this early period.

After the war, the iron industry continued to prosper. In the
mid-nineteenth century Ringwood's mansion was built (1854) and
became the country seat of an iron magnate, Cooper Hewitt.
Hewitt's fortune was estimated to be the sixth largest in America,
and his manor house is suitably grand. (Furnished elegantly and
hung with fine art, including Hudson River school paintings, the
manor is open to the public at certain times—see below.)

Abram Hewitt and his family decided to landscape a portion
of the 33,000 acres of Ringwood. The Hewitts laid out their gardens
by drawing upon classical designs seen during their European travels,

particularly those of Versailles and the Villa d'Este. (What Versailles gardeners accomplished with public taxation, Hewitt wished to create on his own—a truly nineteenth-century American aim!) Hewitt and his gardeners set out formal and informal gardens, allées, terraces, and walls—all adorned with sculpture of various origins, some still mysterious. Large areas of pristine landscape were left in natural state to emphasize the dramatic hilltop views.

Unlike many more modern sculpture parks, Ringwood gardens are home to many incidental marble ornamental sculptures and wrought-iron "confections," rather than primarily settings for art. As in so many European gardens, each sculpture is an integral part of plantings, vistas, and stone-walled enclosures. These intimate spots are intriguing and inviting; each has its own benches and low walls for resting and contemplation.

There are no tags, no labels for identifying the art. Instead you may simply enjoy the odd stone sphinxes that seem to be some sort of motif (Mrs. Hewitt had several of them copied from the sphinxes at the Louvre), nymphs, and sculptured heads as vaguely "classical" and curiously fitting to their surroundings. A classical statue representing Asia is at one end of the main axis of the formal gardens; her counterpart, *Africa,* is now gone. (Both reportedly came from the bishop's palace at Avignon in France.) You'll see wrought-iron works all around the manor house as well, and though these are abstract and ornamental, they seem perfectly appropriate to an iron magnate's home. Among them are a pair of iron lanterns in front of the house that came from the governor's mansion in New York. There are also three of the four lanterns that lit the colonial statue of King George in Bowling Green.

A particular oddity is the geometrically divided, stone-walled, and terraced hillside above the manor. (The visitor can stroll everywhere at Ringwood, and children will enjoy walking along the low, flat-topped walls.) One of the most intriguing of these areas is near the mansion, where a grove of straight and evenly spaced trees create an allée in which a series of identical torchères is laid out. (Their origin was Colonnade Row in New York City.)

Giving the impression of a vast green chessboard, this spot is as eccentric as the giant iron gates that do not seem to lead anywhere in particular at the edge of the crystal lake below the house. (In fact, Hewitt, who purchased them from his alma mater, Columbia University, used them to mark the original site of the road used by the Continental Army from West Point to Morristown.) In any case, like the art throughout the estate, the gates serve to punctuate and ornament the landscape.

Woods and woodland trails surround the gardens. There are a few picnic tables set with grand vistas in mind. In an outing at Ringwood, you can combine nature's wonders with formal gardens, sculpture, and European landscape design.

✻ **Admission:** Fee for parking in season.

Garden open: Year-round. The gardens are particularly inviting in spring and summer. Visitors in parts of December and April can tour the house as well as the grounds.

Further information: Ringwood Manor is part of Ringwood State Park, which offers swimming, fishing, boating, and hiking in season. Information on facilities and hours can be obtained at the above number. The Skylands Botanical Garden is nearby. You may want to combine a visit.

Directions: From New York City, take the New York State Thruway to the junction with Route 17 north. Follow signs toward Ringwood, approximately 8 miles from intersection. Just after Shepherd Lake sign, turn right at Ringwood Manor State Park. Additional driving directions are on the Web site.

9. Skylands Botanical Garden

Morris Road, **Ringwood,** N J; (973) 962–9534; www.njbg.org

*S*KYLANDS, New Jersey's state botanical garden, is aptly named. To visit this vast site deep in the Ramapo Mountains, you must drive up and up on a winding road—toward the sky.

Finally you reach what appears to be (and once was) a grand— yet surprisingly informal—country estate, complete with elegant Tudor-style buildings, delightful gardens, long allées, and broad vistas. The beautifully designed landscape combines formal and naturalistic areas, separated by a magnificent crab-apple walk; broad, panoramic views; and even pieces of sculpture. The ambience is low-key and friendly. Exploring these spacious grounds is a most pleasant, even joyful experience, particularly on a bright spring day, when the many blooming plants add their enchantment.

Skyland's origins as a gentleman's working farm are still apparent in its rustic yet genteel charms. Francis Lynde Stetson, a prominent turn-of-the-twentieth-century New York lawyer, called his property Skyland Farms. His grounds (which also included the mansion, sweeping lawns, and even a small golf course) were designed by Samuel Parsons Jr., a protégé of Frederick Law Olmsted.

But it was the estate's next proprietor, Clarence McKenzie Lewis, who was responsible for turning Skylands into a botanical showplace. Lewis, an amateur but dedicated botanist, collected plants from all over the world during the 1920s. With his army of gardeners, he planted specimens from Afghanistan, Chile, and New Zealand, as well as from New Jersey. Although he engaged landscape architects to design the gardens around the house, he had much to say about which plants should go where. Lewis carefully considered the color, texture, form, and even fragrance of each plant, so that it would be part of a harmonious whole.

In the 1960s New Jersey purchased the property, and in March 1984 the ninety-six acres surrounding the manor house were designated as the state's official botanical garden.

Before setting forth on your walk, you might want to pick up a descriptive guide and map at the visitor center, where the helpful staff will be glad to give you additional information. Among Skyland's many offerings are an Annual Garden, Summer Garden, Azalea Garden, Peony Garden, Lilac Garden, Octagonal Garden, Winter Garden, Magnolia Walk, Crab Apple Vista, Bog Garden, Swan Pond, Wildflower Garden, Heather Garden, a greenhouse collection, and miles of walking to satisfy even the most energetic visitor. The 1920s manor house (made from stone quarried on the estate) can be visited by guided tour only, but you can wander through the broad landscape and individual gardens on your own.

The Winter Garden (which Lewis could enjoy from his library window on even the dreariest wintry day) features a rare collection of thirty varieties of evergreens. Included are an Atlas cedar, a Jeffrey pine (now grown to giant proportions), an Algerian fir, and an impressive Japanese umbrella pine (a main attraction). You can walk around the trees and admire their different shapes, sizes, and shades of green, gray-blue, gray, and even gold.

The nearby formal Terrace Gardens behind the manor house are like individual outdoor galleries. The Octagonal Garden, so named for its central pool and fountain, includes a charming rock garden; the gracious Magnolia Walk, with its fragrant plantings, leads to the Azalea Garden, resplendent with banks of azaleas and rhododendrons on both sides of a reflecting pool. Beyond lie the Summer, Tree Peony, and Lilac Gardens. A good place to take a short rest to plot your next route is on a semicircular stone bench at the end of a grouping of hemlocks in the Peony Garden.

The Crab Apple Vista—an incredible double row of trees that forms the boundary between the gardens near the house and the wilder areas to the east—is undoubtedly Skyland's most enchanting attraction. As you walk on this half-mile stretch, surrounded on each side by more than 160 crab apples (whose spring blossoms alone are worth the trip!), you can enjoy wide views of gardens, meadows, woods, and mountains. At the end of the vista, you'll find the Four Continents statues, opposite the Horsechestnut Collection. Set in a semicircle next to the woods, these time-worn stone forms represent the four continents (minus Australia). Their style is classical with romantic overtones, and they are based on seventeenth-century works.

From here you can wander through the more informal collections to see rhododendron, heather, and different varieties of wildflowers; nearby is Swan Pond, where you are more likely to come upon frogs than anything else.

You'll find there is more to discover and do at Skylands than simply a day stroll through the gardens. Special events and classes in horticulture, nature photography, and nature watercolor painting offer the opportunity to experience Skylands from different perspectives.

✺ **Admission:** Fee during summer.
　　Garden open: Daily from dawn to dusk.
　　Further information: Tours available daily every half hour from April through October.
　　Directions: From the New York State Thruway or Route 4, take Route 17 north. Follow signs for Ringwood just after Shepherd Lake on Morris Avenue.

10. Colonial Park

Elizabeth Avenue, **Somerset,** NJ; (732) 873–2459;
www.park.co.somerset.nj.us

*T*HERE ARE TWO GARDENS here of major interest. This extraordinary pair of gardens—one all roses, the other a fragrance
and sensory garden—is something special. While Colonial Park
forms only a small, one-acre part of a large and spacious county park
in Franklin Township, it has a rare quality all its own. Once part of
a private estate, the gardens were developed by a horticulturalist
when they became part of the public park.

The unusual of the two gardens is the fragrance and sensory
garden. Newly designed with braille plaques and a low handrail, this
garden includes especially interesting flowers and plants to smell and
touch. Each example has an unusual quality, such as the soft and
fuzzy lamb's ear, the fragrant lavender, and the tasty mint. As you
make your way around the garden, you can feel and smell and even
taste these odd, fragrant plants and then guess what they are or read
the small plaques. There are soft, spongy plants; prickly plants; and
aromatic lemony plants. The flat walkway is made to accommodate
the handicapped and visually impaired, and flagstone paving and
intersecting strips of brick indicate changes in direction. There are
many charming arbored benches for resting. We recommend this
walk for families with children, as it is quite short.

Adjoining the sensory and fragrance garden is the rose garden,
and what a rose garden it is! Described as "an encyclopedia of roses,"
the collection includes 4,000 rosebushes (275 varieties) that bloom
from early June all the way into fall. One of the sections is called
Grandmother's Garden, which contains old hybrid perpetual and
hybrid tea roses, while the Dutch Garden is in the style of a formal
rose garden in Holland. It is a beautifully designed garden that is
constantly in bloom during the long season. Everything is identi-

fied. A walk through it on the flagstone walks can be interrupted with little rests on arbored benches. For the rose fancier this is a blissful stroll.

If you are of a romantic disposition, you'll find as we did that both gardens have a touch of another time and place about them, especially on a hot summer day, with flowery aromas wafting through the air, and the cool shaded benches inviting you to rest for a moment.

❀ **Admission:** Free.

Garden open: Daily 10:00 A.M. to 8:00 P.M. from June to November.

Further information: Colonial Park is a vast park, rather overdeveloped, with something for everyone seeking recreation, from paddleboats to a small forestry nature walk, a nice lilac garden, picnic tables, tennis courts, and a playground, in addition to the gardens described above. There are other walks in the park of course, including a stroll through the arboretum. Guided tours are available.

Directions: From I–287 take exit 12 at Weston Canal Road. Go south on Canal Road. Turn left before the bridge and continue alongside the canal. Turn left onto Weston Road, then right onto Mettlers Road. Follow signs for the park.

11. Doris Duke Gardens

Route 206, **Somerville**, N J; (908) 722–3700;
www.njskylands.com/atdukgar.htm

$\mathcal{D}$URING THE COLD WINTER MONTHS, no outing is more cheerful than visiting these splendid interconnected hothouses about an hour from New York. The Duke Gardens are part of the estate of Doris Duke, the tobacco heiress, and are one of New Jersey's major attractions. From the moment you drive through the imposing iron gates with their black eagles on top, you feel as if you have entered a magical world of free-roaming deer, exotic flowers, and mythical trees. The fact that you are picked up at the entrance in a van and transported to this fantasy environment adds to the special ambience.

The conservatories are surrounded by acres of woodsy parkland, with trees planted in formal rows, reminiscent of a European estate. The greenhouses themselves, built in the late nineteenth century for family use, are beautiful. Their ornate glass structure is in an Edwardian conservatory style that is carried into several of the indoor gardens.

The full acre of display gardens was opened to the public in 1964. The Duke family maintains strict control over the management of the estate, and there any many regulations to protect the environment and the valuable plants.

Each of the eleven hothouses has a different theme. You walk from one to the next (in the company of a knowledgeable guide and several other visitors) in about one hour's time. These are total landscape environments that follow the traditions of various countries and eras. There are statuary, rock paths, bridges, and pagodas, as well as a profusion of exotic flowers, shrubs, and trees.

The first stop, the Italian garden, is a wonderful beginning. It includes luxuriant blooms of mimosa, bird of paradise, orange and pink bougainvillea, Italian statuary and fountains, gravel paths, and an aura of nineteenth-century romance.

From there you go to the American colonial garden, more orderly and classical, with well-groomed hedges, baby's tears ground cover, camellia bushes, huge rounded magnolias, and hanging pink and white petunias. White latticework and brick-trimmed paths add to the colonial flavor.

The next conservatory—the Edwardian garden—is filled with orchids of every size and brilliant color. White, purple, and magenta blossoms are set off by the deep green of rubber plants and palms in the warm, humid surroundings. The orchids are supplied by other greenhouses on the grounds. This is the quintessential garden of turn-of-the-twentieth-century romantic novels.

The formal French garden is next. Eighteenth-century lattice-work surrounds this charming formal arrangement of stone paths, niches, ivy-festooned columns, statuary, delicate fountains, and wonderful flowery designs—including a giant fleur-de-lis of brightly colored plants arranged in the style of the gardens of Versailles.

A group of English gardens follows: an herb garden, a rockery, a topiary garden, and a marvelous freestyle annual garden with wonderful color combinations.

Contrasting with this brilliance is the desert garden, with dirt floor and giant cactuses reaching up to the glass ceiling. The ambience is that of the American Southwest: brown and gray-green tones in knobby, fantastic shapes give the visitor the sense of wild, untamed nature.

You then come to the Chinese garden, an oasis of peace and tranquility. Not as colorful as the European-style flower gardens, it is nonetheless one of the most appealing. Rock formations and goldfish in small ponds, delicate arching stone bridges, mysterious grottoes for contemplation, leaning willows, and a zigzag walk to ward off evil spirits are among the engaging aspects of this traditional Chinese garden.

The Japanese garden is more stylized, with elegant teahouse, tiny running streams, miniature wood bridge, contemplation area with carefully raked soil to represent waves, and the classic gnarled tree forms of Japanese landscape.

An impressive Indo-Persian garden comes next. The most striking feature is its geometric design, from the patterned cutout white walls and long reflecting pool to the crisp designs made by the yellow, orange, and white flowers and citrus trees. Although it represents an Islamic summer palace garden, it seems like an illustration to a fairy tale.

The tropical rain forest garden is a mass of jungle plants of many different sizes and shapes of green, with an occasional lady's slipper orchid hidden in the foliage. Spanish moss, banana plants, and huge elephant ears proliferate.

The semitropical garden in the Mediterranean style is the last. Many kinds of purple flowers decorate the edges of the brick paths and terrace, while gloxinias and gardenias in large urns and hanging bougainvillea add brilliant color to the gray-green ferns. Your own garden might seem very pale after this visit!

✤ **Admission:** Fee.

Garden open: Daily noon to 4:00 P.M. from October through March; additional tours on Wednesday and Thursday 8:30 to 10:30 P.M.

Further information: This is a walk that we highly recommend for all adults, including the elderly. Although the walk is not difficult, you are advised to wear flat shoes, as the footing is sometimes awkward over occasional rocky paths. We do not suggest that you bring children, unless they are particularly interested in plants. It is definitely a decorous walk in which everything is rare and special. Cameras are not allowed, nor should you touch anything. There are no eating or drinking facilities, nor are there picnic grounds.

To visit the gardens you must make advance reservations. Call about a week in advance. You are not allowed to wander at will but must accompany a tour (limited to ten people).

Directions: From I–287 south, take exit 17 at the junction with Route 206 south to the Somerset Shopping Center. The gardens are located 1 ¼ miles south of the shopping center, with the entrance on the right.

Don't Miss . . .

12. Willowwood Arboretum

Longview Road, **Gladstone,** N J; (973) 326–7600;
www.parks.morris.nj.us/parks/wwmain.htm

THIS 130-ACRE ARBORETUM, named for its extensive collection of willows (more than one hundred kinds), also features wonderful oaks, maples, ferns, and wildflowers. In spring cherries, magnolias, and lilacs add their delicate color to the site. Although there are two small formal gardens, including the Cottage Garden with neatly planted vegetables and flowers in rectangular beds, the overall feeling at Willowwood is one of delightful informality and eclecticism. Once a working farm (from the mid-1700s to the early 1900s), the land was later cultivated to grow collections of distinctive plants— a passion of the new proprietors in 1908, the Tubbs brothers. The grounds include the eighteenth-century residence and a number of old barns set amid grassy, mowed paths. A small stone bridge in the Japanese style will take you across a pretty stream that runs through much of the land. Among other Oriental touches to note are a katsura tree, Japanese primrose, and clumps of bamboos. A descriptive trail guide (available at the entrance) will lead you through the arboretum, or you can ramble about at will.

❁ **Admission:** Free.
Garden open: Daily.

13. Grounds for Sculpture

18 Fairgrounds Road, **Hamilton,** N J; (609) 586–0616;
www.groundsforsculpture.org

SCULPTURE PARKS seem to be proliferating in the Mid-Atlantic
region, as more people discover the joys of viewing art in natural
settings. One of the most striking recent additions to these outdoor
museums is Grounds for Sculpture. Situated on twenty-two acres on
the edge of a small lake—once the site of the New Jersey State Fairgrounds—it includes a handsome, airy building for displaying indoor
sculpture and the surrounding park. The often bold, contemporary
outdoor pieces, placed with great care for visual interaction with
their national environment, appear in grassy expanses and courtyards, amid impeccably tended trees, shrubs, and flower beds. The
permanent collection is complemented by works on temporary
display (there are three exhibits each year). A picturesque lotus
pond and gazebo (where you can sit, have a snack, and enjoy the
view), a graceful iron arbor (a remnant from the past) with climbing wisteria, a pergola, and a colonnade add unusual appeal to this
inviting site.

The park opened in 1992 and was the creation of the sculptor
J. Seward Johnson Jr., who was also the driving force behind the
adjacent Johnson Atelier, foundry, and art school. In fact, one of the
most original works on permanent exhibit is this artist's witty three-
dimensional retake of Manet's seminal painting *Déjeuner sur l'herbe*.
Appropriately called *Déjeuner Déjà Vu,* its lifelike figures sit in
secluded splendor on the edge of a small, woodsy pond.

Whether your interests are artistic or botanic—or both—you
will enjoy a stroll through Grounds for Sculpture.

✿ **Admission:** Free.

Garden open: Friday, Saturday, and Sunday 10:00 A.M. to 4:00 P.M.; by
appointment Tuesday through Thursday 9:00 A.M. to 4:00 P.M.

14. Lambertus C. Bobbink Memorial Rose Garden

Thompson Park, 805 Newman Springs Road,
Lincroft, N J; (732) 842–4000;
www.monmouthcountyparks.com/parks/thompson.asp

WITHIN THOMPSON PARK, with its 665 acres of playing fields, tennis courts, a lake, fitness trails, and activity centers, lies the surprisingly intimate Lambertus C. Bobbink Memorial Rose Garden.

This pretty garden was created in the 1970s by Dorothea Bobbink White in memory of her father, the dean of commercial rosarians in America. It is an outdoor art gallery dedicated to the rose, displaying prize-winning varieties that have been evaluated in test gardens around the country. Included are some 1,500 plants, all labeled and documented. An accompanying flyer indicates the latest plants—some bear such unlikely names as "Living Easy," "Mr. Lincoln," "Brass Band," "Hot n' Spicey," and "Voodoo"—along with a complete and systematic description of each. Anyone interested in learning more about roses will find a visit here informative and appealing.

The garden is arranged with artistic flair, enclosed within a relatively small space. Flower beds in unusual zigzag shapes contrast with rounded gazebos graced with climbing roses. The abundant roses appear in different shades of red, pink, yellow, and white, creating a vivid and colorful tableau. This is a quiet spot in which to enjoy some of nature's pleasures. The park offers classes, walks, and demonstrations about plants, as well as many other programs and events.

❁ **Admission:** Free.
Garden open: Daily 8:00 A.M. to dusk.

15. Prospect Garden

Princeton University Campus, **Princeton,** NJ; (609) 258–3455;
www.facilities.princeton.edu/prospect

THIS SERENE FLOWER GARDEN is situated within the Princeton University campus. Aptly named Prospect for its views to the east, the property includes a nineteenth-century Florentine-style mansion and gardens. The latter are circular in design, with beds of perennials and annuals surrounding a central fountain. Around the formal plantings are carefully tended lawns and evergreens. It is easy to see why this romantic spot is often used for wedding parties as well as for traditional outdoor university functions.

In the late 1870s, the once-private estate was presented to the university to be used as the residence of its president. (It remained as such until 1968). Its first occupant, President McCosh, often compared it to the Garden of Eden for its idyllic charms. When Woodrow Wilson became president of the university, he enclosed five acres of the then much vaster grounds with an iron fence; this was done to keep unruly undergraduates from trampling the flower beds on their way to class! Mrs. Wilson rearranged much of the garden and planted the evergreens in the background that you see today.

If you're visiting in the Princeton area, you won't want to miss Prospect Garden, particularly in June, when its roses are in full bloom.

❀ **Admission:** Free.
Garden open: Daily from dawn to dusk.

16. Waterford Gardens

East Allendale Road, **Saddle River**, N J; (201) 327–0721; www.waterford-gardens.com

THE CONCEPT of the water garden—with its trickling falls, ponds of blooming water lilies, rocks, and reeds—is increasingly popular among home gardeners. A commercial but very tasteful enterprise in Bergen County, Waterford Gardens has display gardens of watery splendor. Here you can walk around a series of brooks and streams, ponds, and falls and see how a water garden is put together with a little help from nature. (There is in fact a real river running through the property.) The company has vast greenhouses growing the different types of water plants in a spectacularly humid indoor environment, and it also offers a conservatory filled with decorative fish. The oddest things about Waterford Gardens are the almost life-size solid skeletons of topiary animals scattered throughout the gardens; from a distance you'd think a small herd of elephants and a llama (or something) are truly grazing in their watery habitat.

❀ **Admission:** Free.

Garden open: Monday through Saturday 9:00 A.M. to 5:00 P.M., 8:00 A.M. to 5:00 P.M. in growing season; Sunday 9:00 A.M. to 4:00 P.M. Closed on major holidays. Best to visit after May.

17. Leaming's Run Gardens

1845 Route 9 north, **Swainton**, N J; (609) 465–5871; www.leamingsrungardens.com

IF YOU'RE EN ROUTE to or from Cape May or other points on the southern shores of New Jersey, you might wish to see Leaming's Run Gardens and its Colonial Farm. Self-described as the largest annual garden in the United States, this thirty-acre site features some twenty-

five intimate gardens—reminiscent of old-fashioned flower beds—
that are replanted each year. Since blossoms appear throughout the
growing season, from early May to October, what you see depends
on when you come. (We saw mostly pansies, begonias, and irises
when we visited in May.) These gardens are a celebration of color
more than anything else, and many are named accordingly, such as
the Blue and White Garden and the Orange Garden. The setting
is woodsy and rustic, including a stream (the original Leaming's
Run) with small wooden bridges, a reflecting water lily pond, and
many varieties of ferns. It is not surprising that you experience déjà
vu on a walk here: A circuitous path winds around like a labyrinth,
taking you from one garden vista to the next and back again, so that
you see the same spot more than once—but from a different angle.
You are asked (through a series of little signs along the path) to
admire certain views from designated vantage points, and from a
waterside gazebo, you are challenged to locate five visible gardens.
There are garden benches throughout from which to view the
surroundings.

At the rustic Colonial Farm (which you eventually reach along
the path), you can learn about the origins of Leaming's Run, once
a 320-acre plantation operated by whalers. (It's hard to imagine
that this part of New Jersey was in fact a whaling center during the
late seventeenth century!) If you have children in tow, they might
enjoy the farm animals, especially the chickens and very vocal roos-
ter. You can also follow a map and read about the gardens in a
brochure available at the gift shop, oddly enough located near the
end of your walk.

Bird-watchers take note: Leaming's Run is famous for its
hummingbirds (especially in August), so bring along binoculars.

❀ **Admission:** Fee.

Garden open: Daily 9:30 A.M. to 5:00 P.M. from mid-May to mid-
October.

Gardenwalks in New York

The primary law of every work of art, namely that it shall be framed upon a single, noble, motive, to which the design of all its parts, in some more or less subtle way, shall be confluent and helpful. . . .

— FREDERICK LAW OLMSTED AND CALVERT VAUX

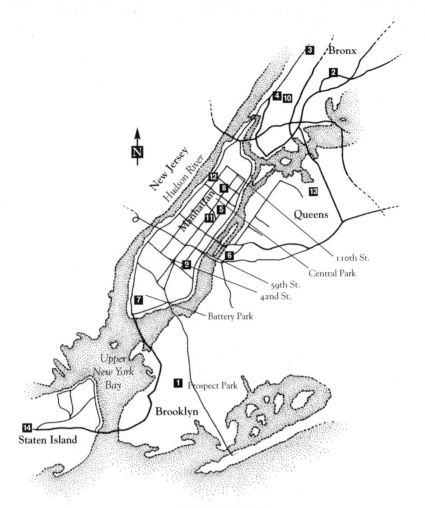

NEW YORK CITY

1. Brooklyn: Brooklyn Botanic
   Garden
2. Bronx: New York Botanical
   Garden
3. Bronx: Wave Hill
4. Manhattan: The Cloisters
5. Manhattan: The Frick Gardens

Don't Miss . . .

6. Long Island City: The Noguchi
   Museum and Sculpture Garden
7. Manhattan: Battery Park City
   Esplanade

8. Manhattan: The Central Park
   Conservancy Garden
9. Manhattan: Ford Foundation
   Garden
10. Manhattan: Fort Tryon Park
11. Manhattan: Mount Vernon
    Hotel Museum and Garden
12. Manhattan: West Side
    Community Garden
13. Queens: Queens Botanical
    Garden
14. Staten Island: Snug Harbor
    Cultural Center

NEW YORK CITY

1. Brooklyn Botanic Garden

1000 Washington Avenue, **Brooklyn**, NY; (718) 623–7200;
www.bbg.org

*T*HE BROOKLYN BOTANIC GARDEN is one of those surprises
you happen upon in New York. In the midst of busy urban
sprawl, around the corner from a dreary stretch of Flatbush Avenue
(but near the lovely Prospect Park), you enter the iron gates of the
Brooklyn Botanic Garden. There you find yourself in an enchanting, colorful, and completely intriguing world of planned gardens,
elegant walkways, weeping cherry trees, and the many sights and
smells of the world's most inviting gardens. The area was reclaimed
from a waste dump in 1910. It takes up some fifty acres (but seems
much larger), and you can walk among the property quite randomly,
from the Japanese paths along a lake to the former rose gardens, from
the Shakespeare Garden to the excellent conservatories. There are
many pleasures in these fifty acres, particularly if you take this outing in the spring.

Every season highlights a different area or style of garden, but
surely April, May, and June are the most colorful times to visit, when
the ornamental trees, luxuriant roses, and many spring flowers are
in bloom. But the rock garden is ablaze with flowers during the
entire growing season, and different species of roses bloom through
September. A fragrance garden, labeled in braille, is another fine section of the gardens; it too is open during the spring, summer, and fall.

All of the plants are labeled, and there are more than 12,000
of them. The conservatories and outdoor gardens include plants
from almost every country in the world. If your taste is for literary

references, you can enjoy the Shakespeare Garden, where plantings are related to passages from the Bard's works. If you want to meditate, you might choose to sit along the banks of the Japanese Garden's lovely walkways. If you are a horticultural fan, there is a section with local flora and many interesting displays of temperate, rain forest, and desert plants.

Sometimes described as "many gardens within a garden" (there are fourteen specialty gardens, many linked along a winding stream), the Brooklyn Botanic is one of the nicest places to spend a day in the city. (You can even eat in one of the gardens.) You'll find it a unique blending of intimacy and grandeur that brings to mind the fine gardens of England rather than the wilder acres of the Bronx Botanical Garden of Central Park.

At the two main entrances to the botanic garden (on Washington Avenue), you can pick up a useful map, which will point you in the right direction. A good place to begin your walk is the Herb Garden, near the parking lot. This charming contoured plot contains more than 300 carefully labeled herbs that have been used for medicine and cooking since the Middle Ages. Intricate Elizabethan knots form an intriguing pattern amid the plantings and add a unique element to this garden. From here you can take a lower or an upper walkway. The upper path will lead you to the Overlook, bordered by ginkgo trees and to the grassy terrace known as the Osbourne Section, where a promenade of green lawns with stylishly shaped shrubs and freestanding columns await you. The pleasant, leafy lower lane will take you past groupings of peonies, crab apple trees, and wisterias to the Cherry Esplanade. We recommend you see this garden in late April or early May, when the deep pink blossoms of the 'Kwanzan' cherry trees are a breathtaking dreamlike pastel. The trees are arranged in rows alongside tall, red-leaved varieties of Norway maples, whose dark leaves create a wonderful contrast in color.

The adjacent Cranford Rose Garden, with its 900 varieties (more than 5,000 rosebushes strong) is the third largest rose garden in the country. In this acre of pure enchantment, you can identify the roses and study them carefully or simply enjoy the overall quality of their beauty.

On the hillside behind a wooden fence is the Local Flora Section, an unusual and less frequented garden. In these two secluded acres the nine ecological zones found within a 100-mile radius of the botanic garden have been re-created in diorama-like form. Serpentine rock, dry meadow and stream, kettle pond, bog, pine barrens, wet meadow and stream, deciduous woodland, border mound, and limestone ledge habitats are displayed with their corresponding flora and rock formations. This rare outdoor classroom is meant for serious observers and nature lovers (school groups are not invited) who want to spend time carefully examining the one hundred or so plant varieties indigenous to this area, such as ferns, phlox, grasses, magnolias, pines, rhododendrons, larches, oaks, heathers, persimmon trees, mosses, and dogwoods. If you wish to study the plants further, you can pick up a guide called *Local Flora Section,* available at the bookstore, since the plants in this garden are not labeled.

From the Local Flora Section, walk down the hill, past the "hedgewheel," a whimsical composition of eighteen different hedging plants (boxwood, viburnum, holly, and yew) to the lovely rock garden on your right. Here rounded glacial boulders define the site, which is planted with contour evergreen shrubs, different types of ground cover, and flowering plants that provide a vivid palette of color for much of the year. Along the path are clumps of spring bulbs, honeysuckles, and forsythias. You'll walk past a bed of barberries that contains twenty varieties, from exotic bamboolike plants to delicate specimens with dainty red and yellow buds. A stream meanders by, flanked by weeping willows, adding to the effect of a romantic English garden.

Eventually you will come to the conservatory complex (called the Steinhardt Conservatory). Here three new, beautifully designed greenhouses contain a rich collection of tropical, temperate, and desert plants, including 3,000 pounds of cacti and succulents brought from the Arizona desert. Throughout the year you can enjoy wonderful flower displays as well as the permanent collection of palms, ferns, and exotic specimens that grace these pavilions. We particularly liked a grotto (in the Tropical Pavilion) carved out of granite and filled with ferns, and the Aquatic House, containing two pools and various plants according to natural habitat. You can view the deeper pool from two perspectives: at the Aquatic House, where you look down on it, or from windows in the Exhibition Gallery on the lower floor, where these unusual aquatic plants can be examined from an angle people rarely see. One gallery is devoted to bonsai, and you can admire the prized collectors' items (some date from the 1920s) in their many varieties, from the most upright to surprisingly naturalistic styles. The curious and intricate art of dwarfing plants is carefully explained and described. The resulting "tray" gardens are real miniature versions—down to the last detail—of regular pines, bamboos, maples, or elms. While you are within the conservatories, don't miss the Exhibition Gallery in the central lower level. It features horticultural displays and art exhibits relating to plants in an atrium-like space. On a recent visit we enjoyed seeing a show called My Garden, a group of alabaster flowers in sensuous configurations by the English sculptor Diana Guest.

Outside the conservatories, next to two reflecting pools, is the elegant Victorian Palm House, once the main conservatory. This lovely old building (now used for special gatherings) adds a dash of turn-of-the-twentieth-century glamour to the complex. Nearby is the administration building, the focus of the many educational and research programs conducted by the botanic garden. Workshops, lectures, exhibits, concerts, films, and classes on just about anything relating to plants are held here. In addition, there is an herbarium (which includes 250,000 dried plant specimens), a plant shop and bookshop, and a horticultural reference library.

The Magnolia Plaza, just outside the administration building, a terrace where more than eighty magnolia trees bloom in May, is formally designed with concentric circular and linear paths. The path to your right (as you face the plaza) will take you to the Fragrance Garden, a delightful, intimate spot that is a pleasure to the senses. Here plants labeled in braille can also be identified through touch and smell.

You'll find the Shakespeare Garden off to the east of the pathway. The tiny signs not only identify the plants but indicate Shakespeare's references to each flower. This is great fun for those of us who remember our plays and sonnets. For those who don't, a guide available at the bookshop will add to your pleasure. The guide includes nice illustrations of Elizabethan gardens and has a full map, noting where to find such flowers and apt quotations as "I think the king is but a man, as I am. The violet smells to him as it doth to me" (*Henry V*); "For though the camomile, the more it is trodden on, the faster it grows, yet youth, the more it is wasted, the sooner it wears" (*Henry IV*); and "What's in a name? That which we call a rose by any other name would smell as sweet" (*Romeo and Juliet*). The garden itself is laid out in a charming, orderly fashion surrounded by a serpentine wall. An oval brick path, a fountain, and a bench contribute to the impression of an English cottage garden of Shakespeare's time.

Finally, you will come to what is arguably the highlight of a visit to the Brooklyn Botanic Garden: the exquisite Japanese Hill and Pond Garden. Designed by Tokeo Shiota in 1914, this prize garden reflects the religious and natural symbolism inherent in Japanese gardens, in which various elements are combined to form a harmonious blend of beauty and peace.

✿ **Admission:** Outdoor gardens are free. Fee for the conservatory complex.

Garden open: From May through August: Tuesday through Friday 8:00 A.M. to 6:00 P.M., and weekends and holidays 10:00 A.M. to 6:00 P.M.; from September to April: Tuesday through Friday 8:00 A.M. to 4:30 P.M., weekends and holidays 10:00 A.M. to 4:30 P.M. Conservatory hours are Tuesday through Friday 10:00 A.M. to 4:00 P.M., weekends and holidays 11:00 A.M. to 4:00 P.M.

Further information: Purchase the guide to the Shakespeare Garden at the bookshop.

Directions: Take the Manhattan Bridge, whose continuation in Brooklyn is Flatbush Avenue; stay on Flatbush all the way to the Grand Army Plaza at Prospect Park, and take the rotary three-fourths of the way around to Eastern Parkway, which borders the park. The botanic gardens are immediately after the Central Library building. There is a large parking area (small fee).

2. New York Botanical Garden

200th Street and Southern Boulevard, **Bronx,** NY;
(718) 817–8700; www.nybg.org

A VISIT TO THE New York Botanical Garden in the Bronx, where you are transported to a special world, will lift your spirits at any time of the year. For here, in this wonderful and vast oasis of natural beauty, all sorts of plants and flowers proliferate during much of the year—whether inside the grand conservatory or throughout the acres of meadows, woodlands, ponds, brooks, hills, and gardens.

The New York Botanical Garden—one of the largest and most important botanic institutions in the country—was the creation of Dr. Nathaniel Lord Britton, a young American botanist. While on his honeymoon in England in 1889, he and his bride visited the Royal Botanic Gardens at Kew outside of London. They were so inspired by what they saw that they were able to convince the

Torrey Botanical Club in New York to create a similar public institution for botany and horticulture within the newly formed Bronx Park.

The resulting complex is on a grand scale, encompassing the famous Enid A. Haupt Conservatory as well as a wide variety of outdoor gardens and buildings housing a library, botanical shop, classrooms, and administrative offices. The conservatory, an elegant Victorian greenhouse ambitiously patterned after the Palmer House at Kew Gardens (1844) and the Crystal Palace at Hyde Park in London (1851), has been one of the main attractions of the botanical garden since its beginnings. It was recently renovated (including the refurbishing of 17,000 individual panes of glass), and its many galleries, reflecting pools, courtyards, and magnificent plantings and changing displays again draw thousands of enthusiastic visitors.

Anyone can find something of interest in these gardens—from children and casual strollers, to serious gardeners and students of botany.

The Demonstration Gardens outside the conservatory offer ideas for cultivating home gardens. Among these is a fragrance garden, where you can sit and enjoy deliciously scented flowers; a cutting garden, with seasonal plantings; a vegetable garden specializing in late summer and early fall crops; and the Rodney White Country Garden, which features informal, minimal maintenance native plantings (many of which flower well into the autumn) in a rustic setting.

A walk (or inexpensive trolley ride) leads to other specialty gardens. You'll find peonies (fifty-eight varieties), daffodils, daylilies, tulips, and chrysanthemums proliferating along bordered pathways. There is a compass garden, where the points of the compass are made of granite cobblestones surrounded by Victorian plantings; a children's maze of boulders and fanciful ladybug topiaries; a small, elegant herb garden that displays ninety-two species of European and American herbs; and a fine rock garden, where masses of alpine flowers are interspersed with giant boulders around a picturesque waterfall. There is a native plant garden, with abundant wildflowers growing amid such different environments as forest trees, a limestone outcropping, marshy meadow, and a sandy strip like that of the New Jersey pine barrens.

The formal Bechtel Memorial Rose Garden is a particular pleasure; its geometric designs are formed by crisscrossing paths amid rose beds containing 2,700 examples of more than 200 varieties. Families with children will take pleasure in the Family Garden, where children can plant, cultivate, and harvest flowers and vegetables within a one-and-a-half-acre plot.

Throughout these varied gardens are avenues of bulb displays, hills of daffodils, circular beds of crocuses, and masses of azaleas and lilacs, flowering crab apples, cherry trees, and magnolias—truly a feast to the eye!

You might also want to explore parts of the Hemlock Forest, which cuts through the middle of the garden. This forty-acre virgin woodland is supposedly the only section remaining of the original forest that once covered all of New York City.

After you have taken in all this natural beauty, you might browse in the Shop-in-the-Garden. Also visit the impressive library (open to the public for research) with more than 190,000 volumes of plant science literature, some dating from the thirteenth century. The library is considered one of the best of its kind, befitting one of the world's great centers of plant study.

❁ **Admission:** Fee.

Garden open: Tuesday through Sunday and Monday holidays 10:00 A.M. to 6:00 P.M. from April through October; 10:00 A.M. to 4:00 P.M. from November through March. Library open Tuesday through Thursday noon to 6:00 P.M., Friday noon to 5:00 P.M.

Further information: Twenty-minute tram tours (tickets for sale on the tram), guided walking tours of the gardens and the forest (information at the visitor center), and self-guided family garden tours are available. Free booklets describing the demonstration gardens can be found on-site. There are picnic areas (near Twin Lakes and the Snuff Mill), as well as two cafes. For general information phone (718) 817–8700, for customized group tours call (718) 817–8577, and for garden events call (718) 817–8777.

Directions: From Manhattan take the Bronx River Parkway north, either from the Cross Bronx Expressway (Interstate 95) or from the Triborough Bridge and the Bruckner Expressway (Interstate 278). Follow signs for the Botanical Garden (after the Bronx Zoo). Parking is on the premises (fee).

3. Wave Hill

Independence Avenue and West 249th Street,
Bronx, NY; (718) 549–3200; www.wavehill.org

*W*AVE HILL is one of New York City's less-known gems. Although familiar to some—particularly gardeners in the know—this rare botanical garden/art environmental center comes as a real surprise to most first-time visitors. Its picturesque setting high above the Hudson River (with remarkable views on all sides), its vast rolling lawns dotted with huge old trees and occasional sculpture, its acres of woodlands, and especially its internationally acclaimed gardens make this twenty-eight-acre park a unique spot. And as you stroll by its two stately manor houses set amid the plantings, you'll imagine you're enjoying a day at a private estate, miles away from the city.

In fact, in the past Wave Hill was the country home of several prominent New Yorkers. From the time the first of its two houses was built in 1848 by the jurist William Lewis Morris, it was occupied by illustrious people who often entertained members of New York society. As a boy, Teddy Roosevelt spent a summer here with

his family, where it is said he learned to appreciate nature. William Makepeace Thackeray visited on occasion; Mark Twain lived here from 1901 to 1903 (and even built a tree house on the grounds); and Arturo Toscanini occupied the house from 1942 to 1945. Most proprietors of Wave Hill were interested in preserving the incredible natural site from profiteering land developers and in further enhancing it with both formal and naturalistic landscaping.

The financier George Perkins, who moved in during the 1890s, was particularly instrumental in securing Wave Hill's future. (A conservationist, he also led the movement to preserve the Palisades and organized the Palisades Interstate Park.) He expanded the estate, adding greenhouses, gardens, orchards, pergolas, and terraces. Working with a landscape gardener from Vienna, he created an English landscape–style garden, mingling formal with informal plantings and rare trees and shrubs with more common species. Many of these plantings still remain. In 1960 the Perkins family deeded the estate to New York City to become an environmental center for the enjoyment of everyone.

Today, Wave Hill (also called Wave Hill Center for Environmental Studies) sponsors indoor and outdoor art shows (particularly outdoor sculpture shows throughout the vast grounds), horticultural exhibits, chamber music concerts, drama and arts festivals, and outdoor dance performances.

But, above all, Wave Hill is a place in which to savor a group of extraordinary formal and wild gardens, both indoor and outdoor. Largely the creation of Marco Polo Stufano, the former director of horticulture, these garden rooms (six in number, plus conservatories, greenhouses, and shade borders) are surprisingly intimate, in contrast with the grandeur of the surrounding landscape. The plantings have been designed on a small scale, separated by grassy areas and paths; the result is an inviting and personal environment, in keeping with Wave Hill's tradition as a private estate.

The gardens have been conceived as living and changing environments, rather than as static historic reproductions. Instead of going by the book, Stufano opted for imaginative and "not too thought out" solutions. The results are artistic displays with unconventional combinations, shapes, and unusually vibrant colors. For example, contrary to traditional garden design, brilliant shades of red, orange, and hot pink are sometimes mixed. With color as one of the guiding principles, each of the gardens and conservatories has been planned so that seasonal changes always offer something of visual interest.

The diversity of plants is staggering, including 1,100 classifications of plants and well over 3,000 species. (In the Wild Garden an exuberant collection of pure species from all five continents is displayed.)

But Wave Hill is more than an unusual botanic garden with a wide range of species. From the moment you walk through the gates, past the small parking area, and onto the meandering brick walkway, you know you're in a very special place—for the landscape has a feeling of space, with breathtaking views and grand vistas. At the same time it has intimacy and charm—unlike most institutional botanic gardens—and an atmosphere of peacefulness and ease. On nice days you sometimes see people sitting in the grass or in comfortable wooden chairs scattered about the lawn, enjoying the view. Others may be sketching, photographing, or wandering among the gardens.

Directly in front of the entrance is a nineteenth-century Italianate columned pergola, a perfect lookout point to the Hudson River and the Palisades. To the right of the entrance, on the site of the former rose garden, is an enchanting flower garden. Enclosed by a rustic cedar fence, it is reminiscent of early-twentieth-century American gardens, with such old-fashioned favorites as peonies, roses, clematis, and hydrangeas. Its fourteen symmetrical beds contain vintage plantings as well as modern perennials, annuals, shrubs, bulbs, and exotic varieties. The look is carefree and romantic. You will frequently see people examining the flowers with book (or brochure available on-site) in hand, admiring the colors and artistic combinations.

Behind the flowers are the conservatory and greenhouses, where you can see tender plants from around the world, as well as exotic palms, cacti and succulents, and tropical plants. These indoor gardens are particularly welcoming in winter.

From here you reach an enclosed herb garden, where you can find a great variety of species (well over one hundred) that have been used in cooking, healing, ornamentation, or religious observance through the ages. The protected Dry Garden comes next, featuring plants from the warmer and drier regions of the world; near it is a delightful rock garden with tiny alpine plants and miniature flowers (best seen in late winter and early spring).

Intimate paths along the hillside lead to the Wild Garden, so called because it contains no hybrids. Its inviting nooks are filled with perennials and shrubs of different sizes and shapes arranged in a naturalistic vein. Facing it is one of two trellised pergolas with climbing vines that enclose both the Aquatic Garden and the Monocot Garden. The former is reminiscent of Japanese gardens, with delicate water lilies and ornamental grasses, among other aquatic plants. It is at its best in late summer and through the fall. From the Monocot Garden (which displays a single group of plants in its variations), you can see an expanse of lawns and forests, as well as river views. A ten-acre woodland beyond has been restored with native plants.

As you wander from one garden to the next, you are likely to see contemporary outdoor sculptures in the grassy areas. Most of them are part of temporary exhibits shown for only a few months at a time. Most are installed in such a way as to harmonize with their surroundings.

The works exhibited indoors are also of an environmental nature. They are shown in the two manor houses, Wave Hill House and Glyndor House. The older of these, Wave Hill House, is a handsome nineteenth-century fieldstone building with white shutters, ivied walls, and a vast terrace overlooking the river. Inside are several gallery rooms. Here you can pick up a map of the area as well as literature and brochures relating to exhibits and subjects of horticultural interest. One series of pamphlets gives detailed information on conifers (among the most ancient plants on earth), with a self-guided tour among Wave Hill's varied and rich collection.

❄ **Admission:** Free on weekdays. Fee on weekends.

Garden open: Tuesday through Sunday 10:00 A.M. to 4:30 P.M., to 5:30 P.M. in summer; closed on major holidays. The greenhouses are open 10:00 A.M. to noon and 2:00 to 4:00 P.M.

Further information: We recommend visiting on weekdays, when Wave Hill is free and uncrowded. The park is a joy to visit at any time

of the year, even in winter. For information about special events, telephone the number above.

Directions: Take the West Side Highway (Henry Hudson Parkway) up
to Riverdale. After the Henry Hudson Bridge toll booths, take the
246th Street exit. Drive on the parallel road north to 252nd Street,
where you turn left and go over the highway. Take a left and drive south
on the parallel road to 249th Street and turn right. Wave Hill is straight
down the hill. Limited parking on the grounds and street parking.

4. The Cloisters

Fort Tryon Park, **New York**, NY; (212) 923–3700;
www.metmuseum.org

AMONG THE particularly magical parts of the Cloisters, the
Metropolitan Museum of Art's medieval-style museum in
northern Manhattan, are the gardens. While the pleasures of
visiting the Cloisters' medieval architecture and seeing its exquisite
collection of fine art from the Middle Ages may be well known to
New York's museumgoers, its gardens are in themselves well worth
a special trip. The arcades of five cloisters have been reconstructed
with the original stones and integrated into the museum's architecture; four cloisters surround their own unusual gardens. These
spots are extraordinarily evocative; in fact, it is hard to believe you
have to exit into the twenty-first century when you leave.

Though they are small, as gardens go, they are so filled with
architectural, sculptural, and botanical interest that you might
spend many hours walking round and round, or dreamily sitting on
a bench imagining you are in thirteenth-century France, perhaps,
or a member of a twelfth-century Cistercian order. Medieval music
plays softly in the background as you walk, and of course the art
treasures of this distant past await you in the stone-walled rooms of
the museum.

Two of the cloisters (square-columned walkways that once were parts of monasteries) are enjoyable to visit even out of garden season, for they are in covered areas and the plants are kept flowering throughout the winter. All four cloister gardens are at their best in late spring and early summer, when the flowers are blooming, the herbs bright and green, the espaliers leafy on their trellises. The following thumbnail descriptions should give you an idea of what to expect from each of these (chronologically listed) garden-walks,

The earliest cloister is Saint-Guilhem-le-Désert. Formerly part of a French abbey started by a Benedictine order in A.D. 804, Saint-Guilhem cloister was built in 1206. Its stone pillars are topped by capitals (the decorative carved tops) whose designs are based on the spiny leaf of the acanthus plant. But there are many additional patterns carved on these columns, including a wonderful series of faces, flowers, entwined vines, and elegant foliage. There are small holes drilled into these designs in intricate honeycomb patterns, and no two columns seem the same.

Some of the sculptural decoration can be traced to ancient Roman design (still in evidence in southern France). This cloister surrounds an indoor garden that is planted fully in early spring. When we saw it last in winter, the flowers were potted and neatly arranged. The architectural details occasionally seem to imitate the very shapes of the leaves and flowers.

Almost directly across the central room from the Saint-Guilhem-le-Désert cloister is the wonderful Saint-Michel-de-Cuxa cloister, a beautiful spot both in winter and in spring and summer, when it is ablaze with flowers. This cloister was in a Benedictine abbey first built in 878 in an area northeast of the Pyrenees. The cloister itself is from the twelfth century. It forms the central part of the framework of the Cloisters museum and is appropriately gracious and inviting. Its original function as a communal place for monks to walk, meditate, read, or take part in processionals can be readily imagined. The lovely stone walks surrounded by archways and columns open onto a sunlit garden of individual bedded flowers and plants. Each column is carved with typically medieval gargoyles, two-headed animals, or two-bodied monsters. You will want to spend time examining this garden and its cloisters, and perhaps sitting on a bench enjoying the ambience of quiet and beauty.

On the lower level of the museum you'll find the Bonnefont cloister, a purely outdoor garden walkway. Its origins are in the south of France, near Toulouse. The cloister, with its slender graceful columns in rows of twos, comes from the late thirteenth/early fourteenth century. Cistercian monks once walked through these cloisters, and the simple design of the architecture and limited amount of sculptural pattern represent their ascetism. Of particular garden interest is the herb garden, a favorite of New Yorkers. More than 250 species of plants that were grown in the Middle Ages are cultivated in this outdoor space. In the center is a charming little well. The herbs are grown in raised planting beds with fences around each bed. Among our particular favorites are the trained espaliers growing against lattices in the sunlight. Anyone with an interest in gardening will find this cloister irresistible.

Finally, the fourth cloister, also on the lower level, is the Trie cloister, from a Carmelite building in the Bigorre region of southern France. Reassembled with parts of several other cloisters, this small outdoor garden arcade is of particular interest if you look at the Unicorn Tapestries in the museum. The garden contains samples of the very plants woven into the design of the tapestries some five centuries ago. (Information at the cloisters will identify the plants for you.) Part of the charm of this garden is the sight of the red tile roof surrounding it and the fruit trees set among the flowers. This garden is only cultivated during growing months.

Though obviously you will get more pleasure out of this medieval gardenwalk in the growing season, even in wintertime it is nice to wander about the unkempt cloisters outdoors, to see the view of the Hudson River, and to contemplate the beauty of the architecture and sculptural designs in the indoor gardens.

Among the many treasures you will want to enjoy in the museum while you are there are the Unicorn Tapestries, the stained glass in the Boppard Room, the wonderful altarpiece by the fifteenth-century painter Robert Campin, and our particular favorites, the medieval wood sculptures. Children, by the way, will enjoy this walk; there are numerous crenellated walls, dark staircases, and impressive and picturesque statues that they'll love, and the observant will notice the medieval playing cards on display.

A visit to the Cloisters is perhaps the closest you can get to being in France while in Manhattan. We found the combination of art, history, and flowering plants an irresistible delight.

✿ **Admission:** Fee.

Garden open: Tuesday through Sunday 9:30 A.M. to 5:15 P.M. from March to October; Tuesday through Sunday 9:30 A.M. to 4:45 P.M. from November to February. Closed New Year's Day, Thanksgiving, and Christmas.

Further information: Many events of interest are held at the Cloisters; among them are gallery talks on medieval imagery, tapestries, gardens of the Middle Ages, and colors in use in medieval France. There are many concerts of medieval music played on early instruments. You will also find demonstrations of how medieval art was made, including such techniques as enameling and miniature painting. There is a guide to the gardens in which each plant is labeled and described. For information on events, including guided tours, call (212) 923-3700. If you feel the need for additional exercise, you might wish to leave the Cloisters by way of Fort Tryon Park and walk south through this very pleasant park with its terrific views of the Hudson River and New Jersey's Palisades.

The best time to visit is during the week, when the museum is less crowded (although you might meet groups of schoolchildren at that time).

Directions: By subway: Take the A train to 190th Street and Overlook Terrace; exit by the elevator and walk through the park. By bus: Take the M4 Madison Avenue (Fort Tryon Park—The Cloisters). By car: Take West Side Drive (Henry Hudson Parkway) north to the first exit after the George Washington Bridge. Follow signs. Parking is on the premises.

5. The Frick Gardens

1 East 70th Street, **New York**, NY; (212) 288–0700; www.frick.org

*M*OST VISITORS agree that the Frick Collection is among New York City's most inviting museums. Its exceptional masterworks (by Rembrandt, El Greco, Veronese, Van Dyck, Gainsborough, Turner, Constable, and Fragonard, among many others) are displayed in an unusually appealing, noninstitutional setting, suggesting the grand private estate it once was. The present galleries still seem like living quarters, with elegant furnishings, plantings, freshly cut flowers, and choice artifacts complementing the harmonious decor. And of special interest to us are its two delightful gardens: an indoor courtyard and a small outdoor garden framed by one of the neoclassical facades of the building.

The interior court, formerly an open carriage court, was designed by John Russell Pope, who converted the mansion into a museum in the early 1930s. It has a barrel-vaulted glass roof, an elegant central fountain, Ionic coupled columns, and colonnades. Surrounding the pool are bronze sculptures and marble walkways and a wide assortment of tropical plants and flowering shrubs, which are changed frequently throughout the year. On the bleakest of winter days, you can sit amid the plantings on one of the stone benches and be immensely cheered by this exuberant display.

The outdoor garden, created in the 1970s, was meant to be a temporary site until a new gallery could be built in its place; it has since become a permanent—and major—asset to the Frick. Those who are familiar with the work of the well-known British landscape architect Russell Page (see the write-up about PepsiCo in Purchase, New York) will be able to identify this as one of his designs. Uncluttered simplicity, serenity, and understated elegance best describe the garden. It adheres to Page's view that "all the good gardens I have ever seen . . . were the result of . . . a simple idea developed as far as it could be." He believed that a city garden in particular ought to exude tranquillity, much like an oasis.

In the tradition of Islamic gardens (which were a source of inspiration for Page), a formal water lily pool is at the center of this symmetrically shaped garden, creating the illusion of a larger space. The water level of the pool and its stone edging are virtually flush with the small, rectangular grassy plot surrounding it. A single fountain jet (in typical Page-like restraint) graces the pool; it is turned on only in winter when there is no plant color to provide interest. Around the garden are a rectangular path lined with carefully clipped hedges and narrow borders of roses, azaleas, hydrangeas, and lilies. Climbing ivies and wisterias and a few ornamental trees add a sense of verticality to the design, echoed by the tall city buildings in the background. The overall effect of serenity is a welcome respite from the bustle of Manhattan just beyond the garden gates.

It is not surprising that a visit to the Frick is high on the list of most visitors to New York, whether they love art or gardens.

✿ **Admission:** Fee.

Garden open: Tuesday through Saturday 10:00 A.M. to 6:00 P.M., Sunday 1:00 to 6:00 P.M.; closed Monday and select holidays. *Note:* Children under 10 are not admitted.

Further information: Concerts, special exhibits, and lectures are held throughout the year. Call for information.

Directions: Take the Fifth Avenue bus to Seventieth Street.

Don't Miss . . .

6. The Noguchi Museum and Sculpture Garden

32-37 Vernon Boulevard, **Long Island City,** NY; (718) 204-7088;
www.noguchi.org

THE NOGUCHI MUSEUM and Sculpture Garden is about the best-disguised art center we've discovered on our wanderings through the city. Set into blocks of old warehouses, it appears to be another nondescript, rectangular building, but on closer inspection you'll see the angles of a contemporary building nestling into its triangular city block. Isamu Noguchi (1904–1988) wanted a home for his works that would be congenial to their style and to his concepts of art's relationship to its surroundings. "These are private sculptures," he said, "a dialogue between myself and the primary matter of the universe."

And what you will find at the beautifully renovated museum are some 350 works that demonstrate the great Japanese sculptor's spiritual presence, as well as his evolving use of stone and other natural materials. The walled-off sculpture garden was designed to bring traditional Asian design to the twentieth century. Even today these delicate stone works, trickling water fountains, abstract shapes, and patterns give you the sensation of being very far away from both Manhattan and the present day.

Noguchi was in fact a quintessentially twentieth-century artist. His search was for abstract realities or what he called "the brilliance of matter" that will turn "stone into the music of the spheres." Everywhere—in the rough stone pillars, the delicate marble pieces, the rounded basalt mounds, the intricate black metal abstractions— you sense the sculptor's preoccupation with pure form and its relationship to the space around it. In this setting of careful calm and contemplation, the word *garden* takes on new meaning. Although this is not art that is easy for the layperson to understand, it is nevertheless an experience that will change the way the most unreceptive observer of contemporary art looks at stone. You will have a new idea of how sculpture can both shape its surroundings and become a part of them. A shuttle bus from Manhattan is available.

✿ **Admission:** Fee.

Garden open: Thursday through Monday.

7. Battery Park City Esplanade

South of Chambers Street, **New York,** NY; www.batteryparkcity.org

THOUGH NOT a traditional garden, this riverside landscape was designed by environmental artist Mary Miss. It is an unusual and enchanting way of combining the natural landscape of the Hudson River's dramatic shoreline with an urban and people-oriented design. We recommend a walk through the entire riverside park (from Chambers Street in the north to Battery Park at the tip of Manhattan) for a taste of contemporary urban planning, sculpture, and plantings.

To get to Battery Park City in lower Manhattan, cross West Street (either by overhead walkway or on street level at the traffic light). Turn south and walk on South End Avenue to Albany Street, where you turn once again west, toward the Hudson River. Battery Park City is a planned community of high-rise apartments and parks that face the Hudson River. The designing of artworks to enhance the site has been a part of the project from the beginning, and works by Mary Miss, Ned Smyth, R. M. Fischer, Richard Artschwager, and Scott Burton (among others) are very much in evidence. The Battery Park City Fine Arts Program has become a sort of test laboratory for the combining of architecture, city planning, gardens, and art at a very spectacular site; it is fascinating to view this contemporary version of an ancient idea.

All of the art at Battery Park City was commissioned by the city and was chosen expressly to enhance the site. One of the most important and successful of these commissions is Mary Miss's design for the esplanade at its south end. Her proposal for the shoreline included a lookout, pilings that rise and fall with the river tide, wooden wisteria-covered archways, boardwalks lighted with blue lanterns, and Japanese-style rock gardens. The architect, Stanton Eckstut, and a landscape architect, Susan Child, helped execute her design. While the site art is surely a form of gentrification of the natural shoreline (you can see what the banks originally looked like, just over the fence at the edge), it is a major attempt to balance the sophisticated urban setting on the shore with the Hudson's rather wild and somber coastline. From the top of the curving steel staircase, you can enjoy an extraordinary view of the shapes and patterns of Mary Miss's design, as well as of the city, the river, and New Jersey.

❁ **Admission:** Free.
  Garden open: Daily.

8. The Central Park Conservancy Garden

Fifth Avenue between 104th and 105th Streets, **New York,** NY;
www.centralpark.org

NESTLED INTO a corner of Central Park is one of the city's most cherished garden spaces, where you will find yourself in a garden of great elegance and beauty. The Conservancy Garden on Fifth Avenue was a gift from the Vanderbilt family a century ago. Classically styled with columns, walkways, areas of lawn, flower beds, two fountains, and stairways, this perfectly maintained garden is a delight. You can stroll through its elegant paths, rest among vine-covered trellises, and admire the changing flower displays. Truly an oasis amid the bustle and cement of the city, the Conservancy Garden is a rare, beautifully kept spot.

One of the city's favorite fountains, the Untermeyer Fountain, is a centerpiece of the Conservatory Garden to the north. Made sometime before 1910, the fountain has three whimsical bronze maidens dancing around a single jet of water. It was made by Walter Schott, a German sculptor and portraitist. Its light, airy design is a charming addition to the harmonious spaces and bright colors of the garden. In the Conservatory Garden to the south is a memorial to the author of *The Secret Garden* and *Little Lord Fauntleroy*, the Frances Hodgson Burnett Memorial Fountain. The sculpture surrounding the fountain consists of a small boy playing the flute while a girl holding a seashell listens. A birdbath at her feet spills into a small pool. The fountain was created by Bessie Potter Vonnoh between 1926 and 1937.

❀ **Admission:** Free.
Garden open: Daily until dusk.

9. Ford Foundation Garden

320 East Forty-third Street, **New York,** NY

ALSO IN MANHATTAN, and surprisingly right in Midtown, is the Ford Foundation Building, halfway between First and Second Avenues on the north side of Forty-second Street. (Enter on Forty-third Street.) This tasteful, contemporary glass edifice is constructed around one of New York's most fabulous and spacious interior gardens, a 130-foot-high "greenhouse" that can be enjoyed by employees and visitors alike. All the interior windows in the building look onto the spectacular greenery, rather than onto the usual cityscape. The one-third-acre oasis is a lush combination of tall trees, terraced shrubbery, ground cover, and water plants gracing a tranquil pond. Although there are seasonal outbursts of brilliantly colored blossoms, the garden is mostly a subtle study of different intensities and

shades of green. One can only wish that more urban corporate centers would create such luxuriant green spaces.

✤ **Admission:** Free.
Garden open: Weekdays during office hours.

10. Fort Tryon Park

193rd Street and Fort Washington Avenue, **New York,** NY;
(800) 201–7275; www.hhoc.org/fftp

"WHAT THE ENGLISH CALL A TERRACE . . . the crescent shaped
intermediate space being either a quiet slope of turf, a parterre of
flowers, a picturesque rocky declivity treated perhaps as a fernery or
alpine garden . . ."—this was the plan described by Frederick Law
Olmsted and Calvert Vaux when they proposed turning this spectacular site into a park.

About nineteen years after Olmsted and Vaux created New
York's "crowning jewel"—Central Park—they suggested this hilly
terrain with its glorious Hudson River panorama as a site worth preserving. Their design for the crescent-shaped area in the Inwood
section of the city became Fort Tryon Park. This surprising urban
oasis is still a beautiful example of park design, with colorful gardens
nestled into the highland landscape above the Hudson and afford-
ing a magnificent view of the river and the Palisades beyond. Fort
Tryon Park has in fact been called one of the most beautiful parks
in America.

Inwood is a northern, cliffside section of the city, where about
two-fifths of the land is parkland. At its northern end you'll find the
Cloisters—New York's magnificent medieval museum (with cloister gardens). The sixty-two acres of Fort Tryon Park are landscaped
with terraces, rock gardens, paved walks, benches, and stone archways—and everywhere there are amazing views. This urban design

never intrudes on its panoramic setting: miles of Hudson River vistas to the west, urban landscapes far below to the east. At the southern entrance to the park, a large sloping rock garden is located; a walk through it will lead to the site of the old Fort Tryon (built in 1777). Much of the park area was part of an estate purchased by John D. Rockefeller Jr. and given to the city.

Fort Tryon's gardens are nestled within the terraced hillside. Large flower beds (originally laid out by Olmsted's son) are kept up nicely, with dozens of different plantings blooming throughout the growing season. Perennials such as iris and phlox and heather are intermixed with exotic shrubs and flowering trees. The gardens are informal and inviting; instead of seeming imposed on the land-scape, they fit in with their spectacular surroundings as if they just happened to be there. Which is of course what Olmsted surely had in mind.

A visit to Fort Tryon Park can easily be combined with a visit to the Cloisters. Since this is a city park, we recommend that Fort Tryon Park be visited in daylight hours only, when it is apt to be filled with walkers.

✤ **Admission:** Free.
Garden open: Daily.

11. Mount Vernon Hotel Museum and Garden

21 East Sixty-first Street, **New York,** NY; (212) 838–6878

THIS CHARMING colonial garden adjoins the fine old house (open to the public) that once belonged to a daughter of John Adams. You are welcome to walk around the garden without visiting the museum. Planted in a characteristic eighteenth-century way, this quaint garden is a charming example of America's most decorative style. Influenced by the Dutch idea of patterned gardens surrounded by colonial board fences, the flowering area is delightful. We recommend a visit in springtime, when tulips, crocus, and hyacinth planted within patterns of brickwork and English ivy make this a bright and charming place to visit. (It is particularly astonishing because it is in the middle of a nondescript block of East Side Manhattan, and invisible from the street.) A brick terrace with old-fashioned benches sits above the flower area. On this level is an herb garden. There are trees and shrubs—many of the flowering varieties, whose best blossoms can be seen in May—including mock orange, viburnum, and flowering quince. Under these trees you'll find a profusion of violets and other bright flowers. But all is orderly in the garden, as recommended by early American (and European) gardeners. This is a well-kept garden, despite the harsh city environment, and also a well-kept secret, even among New York natives. A garden map is available at the desk.

❄ **Admission:** Free; there is a small fee to visit the house.
Garden open: Tuesday through Sunday 11:00 A.M. to 4:00 P.M. The museum is closed in August.

12. West Side Community Garden

West Eighty-ninth Street and Amsterdam Avenue, **New York,** NY; www.westsidecommunitygarden.org

ON THE CORNER of Eighty-ninth and Amsterdam in the heart of the Upper West Side is this intimate and charming green oasis. Amid brilliantly colored flowers arranged in circular terraced beds, graceful trellises, shade trees, and small vegetable plots (some tended by local school groups), people of all ages enjoy a quiet respite from the urban scene. To view the gardens up close you can walk on a small path and up wood steps to the different levels of flower beds.

A few random tables and chairs beneath leafy canopies complete the tasteful decor. We only wish that more such inviting spots were scattered about the city!

✿ **Admission:** Free.
   Garden open: Daily.

13. Queens Botanical Garden

43-50 Main Street and Dahlia Avenue, **Queens,** NY;
(718) 886–3800; www.queensbotanical.org

QUEENS BOTANICAL GARDEN is a pleasant thirty-eight-acre park (once a dumping ground), of which about half is dedicated to formal plantings. You'll enjoy the Perkins Memorial Rose Collection (with its more than 4,000 bushes), a rock garden, herb garden, and specialized garden for the blind. In spring, flowering cherry trees, crab apples, and thousands of bright tulips add their magic, while in fall you can enjoy a wonderful display of colorful chrysanthemums. Queens Botanical Garden is a small but attractive spot to visit, with flat terrain for easy walking. The garden also sponsors year-round workshops on such topics as Japanese-style dish gardens and hanging gardens for indoor or outdoor use.

✿ **Admission:** Free.
   Garden open: Daily.

14. Snug Harbor Cultural Center

Richmond Terrace and Snug Harbor Road, **Staten Island,** NY; (718) 448–2500; www.snug-harbor.org

THIS IS A DELIGHTFUL village of historic buildings and gardens—a true find in New York. From its Gothic revival houses to its conservatory and concert hall and outdoor sculpture, Sung Harbor Cultural Center is a wonderful place for a walk and a cultural outing.

As you enter Snug Harbor, you come to the small cottages now used by artists in residence. Opposite the cottages are the greenhouse and the particularly charming flower gardens. The landscape of the entire park is Victorian in feeling, and so are the garden areas. Among the high points of this landscape are the trees, including wonderful willows, and a superb collection of flower gardens. The Staten Island Botanical Garden, which moved to the site in 1975, has put in a variety of small gardens: a formal English perennial garden; a butterfly garden (whose plants are specifically nourishing to butterflies); a Victorian rose garden; an herb garden featuring medicinal and culinary plantings; a white garden, which experiments with vertical plantings; a bog garden; and inside the conservatory the Neil Vanderbilt Orchid Collection. Any garden enthusiast will enjoy the way these small treasures of planting are arranged. Each in its own season is a treat. Tours, lectures, and demonstrations are available at the botanical garden, but you will enjoy wandering on your own.

Of particular charm near the gardens is Snug Harbor's Chinese-style pagoda built by Charles Locke Eastlake of England. This little pavilion is a concert site and additional Victorian touch to the landscape. At the end of the garden is a dark green latticework enclosure, planted with charming flowers, and you can sit on the white wrought-iron benches and enjoy a summer's day. We found it particularly appealing.

Don't miss Snug Harbor's most impressive recent addition: The New York Chinese Scholar's garden. Modeled after the scholar's gardens of the Ming dynasty (1368–1644), this exquisite one-acre garden is the only outdoor example of its kind in the country. its designer—one of China's eminent landscape architects—along with an army of artisans (one hundred in China doing preparatory work on carvings and tiles, and more than forty here) created courtyards, pavilions, a teahouse, and lotus ponds with waterfalls and rocks, reminiscent of the famous Garden for Lingering in Suzhou.

❀ **Admission:** Free; fee for the New York Chinese Scholar's garden.
Garden open: Snug Harbor is open daily dawn to dusk; the gardens are best in spring and early summer. The Chinese Scholar's garden is open Tuesday through Sunday 10:00 A.M. to 5:00 P.M.

HUDSON VALLEY

15. Wethersfield Garden

Pugsley Hill Road, **Amenia**, NY; (845) 373–8037

*T*HERE ARE MANY WAYS in which gardens can be artistic—or appear to be art themselves. Topiary gardens are like parks of living sculpture, while sculpture parks are themselves gardens of art.

At Wethersfield, a country estate near the town of Amenia, you'll find gardens that are at once repositories for sculpture and themselves a kind of spatial work of art. As you walk through the landscaped grounds of Wethersfield, you'll have a sense of trompe l'oeil—that French term for art that plays spatial tricks on the unsuspecting (but delighted) viewer.

Wethersfield's gardens are so artful that the eye can be deceived by the long allées and decorative gates and by the geometric shapes of pruned bushes and trees that form the setting for its marble statuary. The gardens within gardens, the sense of perspective, the care-

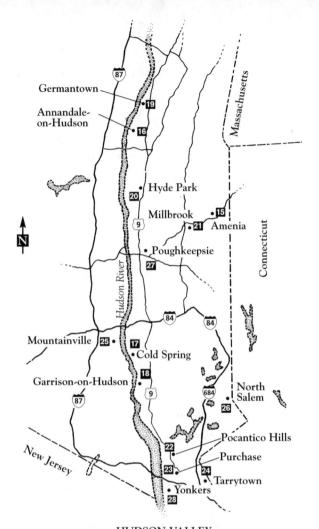

HUDSON VALLEY

15. Amenia: Wethersfield Garden
16. Annandale-on-Hudson:
    Montgomery Place
17. Cold Spring: Stonecrop
    Gardens
18. Garrison-on-Hudson: Boscobel
19. Germantown: Clermont State
    Historic Site
20. Hyde Park: Vanderbilt Mansion
    Gardens
21. Millbrook: Innisfree Garden
22. Pocantico Hills: Kykuit
23. Purchase: The Donald M.

Kendall Sculpture Gardens
at PepsiCo
24. Tarrytown: Lyndhurst

Don't Miss . . .

25. Mountainville: Storm King
    Art Center
26. North Salem: The Hammond
    Museum and Japanese Stroll
    Garden
27. Poughkeepsie: Springside
    Restoration
28. Yonkers: Untermyer Park

fully placed statuary—these reminded us of the surreal gardens of René Magritte's paintings, where a hat may appear over a hedge in a dreamlike green garden of distant proportions and uncertain boundaries.

The gardens are the high point of the visit to this gentleman's country estate (and working farm).

Wethersfield is now open formally to the public. It was the home of Chauncey Stillman, an investor and philanthropist, who purchased it in 1937. The estate currently consists of 1,400 acres. The setting of the house and gardens is magnificent, overlooking a vast panorama of fields and mountains—the Catskills to the west and the Berkshires to the north. The gardens cover more than ten acres of the estate and provide a marvelous place to walk. There are also woodland paths that you can enjoy at your leisure. Leave yourself plenty of time to see them, and even to walk through the woods to the Palladian arches at the edge of the field.

Pick up a map at the upper parking lot, where you leave your car. You'll find the brochures in a basket between two stone lions. The gardens, which you will enter here, are generally neoclassical and French in style. They are simultaneously grand and intimate. You might even see occasional peacocks strolling through them. Each garden is separated from the next by hedges or wrought-iron gates. Though there are formal flower beds, it is the geometric design of borders and flagstone paths, reflecting pools, and green walls of hedges that create the special ambience. Everywhere are cones, balls, columns, and boulder-shaped topiary designs, as well as gargoyles and cherubs, temples, animal sculptures, and classical figures nestling into the greenery and demarcating each individual area.

You'll find a water lily pond with sculptured turtles, deer sculptures by John Flannagan, two Pans by an Englishman named Peter Watts, two nymphs and a Hercules of limestone, some charming recumbent sheep, a naiad by the Swedish sculptor Carl Milles gracing a fountain, and a stone stairway leading to a belvedere with a stunning view of the landscape.

A Polish artist named Joseph Stachura made many of Wethersfield's sculptures, including the Madonna and other religious works around the grounds. They are representational marble carvings that are graciously placed here and there in shrinelike settings.

All of the sculpture is traditional—this is not a venue for the latest in abstract works. Instead, it is a period setting with a strikingly modern sense of space. Like an outdoor gallery, the gardens are a form of three-dimensional art, ornamented with sculpture; the emphasis of the landscape design has surely been on form.

But this is not to say that there are no charming flower beds and wonderful trees. There are in fact a rose garden, perennial gardens, a cutting garden, and many other distinctive sections. (An army of gardeners works year-round.)

❁ **Admission:** Fee.

Garden open: Wednesday, Friday, and Saturday noon to 5:00 P.M. from June through September. To visit the garden, house, or carriage house, you must make an advance reservation.

Further information: The beautiful gardens of Innisfree are nearby.

Directions: Wethersfield is located in northern Dutchess County, New York. From the Taconic State Parkway, take Route 44 north of Millbrook, then take Route 86 (Bangall-Amenia Road) and turn right onto Pugsley Hill Road. Follow signs about 1 ⅓ miles to the entrance on the left.

16. Montgomery Place

River Road, **Annandale-on-Hudson**, NY; (845) 758–5461;
www.hudsonvalley.org/web/mont-main

*M*ONTGOMERY PLACE is one of the great Hudson River estates, combining romantic, sweeping landscaped lawns, woodlands, and magnificent views. This 434-acre site includes a nineteenth-century mansion (open for visitors), a few formal gardens, magnificent trees, and a wide variety of walking trails. Though its formal gardens are not yet spectacular (they are in the process of restoration), the overall landscape of ancient trees, wildflowers, and breathtaking views make a long walk here idyllic.

Described in an 1866 guidebook of the fine estates along this portion of the Hudson as "the most perfect in its beauty and arrangements," Montgomery Place was admired for "waterfalls, picturesque bridges, romantic glens, groves, a magnificent park, one of the most beautiful of the ornamental gardens in this country, views of the river and the mountains, unsurpassed . . ."

Built 1804–05 by a branch of the Livingston family (see their Hudson River estate nearby at Clermont), Montgomery Place was part of a 160,000-acre family holding. The house, designed in the federal style, was remodeled in the 1830s to reflect the elegant lifestyle of the Livingstons of the time.

It was then that the working orchard and farms and commercial nursery became part of a landscape of pleasure grounds. The splendid romantic sweep of the lawns and curving driveways and stone bridges, the plantings of groves of great trees, the variety of settings—these ideas of landscape design were made with the advice of the owners' good friend Andrew Jackson Downing. He described Montgomery Place in his 1859 book as "one of our oldest improved country seats . . . nowhere surpassed in America in point of location, natural beauty, or landscape gardening charms."

The estate stayed in the family's hands throughout the nineteenth century, and the Delafields, descendants of the Livingstons, continued to preserve it. In the 1930s Violetta Delafield, already an amateur botanist and expert horticulturalist (with a specialty in mushrooms) created showplace gardens at the estate that flourished until her death in 1949. For nearly forty years thereafter the gardens declined. Today they are being carefully restored under the direction

of Historic Hudson Valley. Using Delafield's writings, oral history, old photographs, and even plant orders, gardeners and landscape historians are attempting to re-create her spectacularly successful gardens. (If you are interested in such detective-cum-horticultural studies, this is the place for you!)

Montgomery Place is very much a tree enthusiast's estate. There are flowering shrubs (lilacs in profusion in May), dogwoods, magnolias, massive horse chestnuts, maples, beeches, sycamores, and the amazing grove of giant black locust trees that surround the house. The spectacular views range from vistas of the nearby Hudson River below the bluff—seen from the terrace of the mansion and framed by the locust trees—to spots deep in the woods where the cataracts of the Sawkill can be enjoyed as they tumble down to the river. A map of the entire estate is available as you enter, so that you can choose your garden or trail or view. Do not come here solely for flower gardens; Montgomery Place is for those garden enthusiasts who think of landscape itself as a form of garden.

✱ **Admission:** Fee.

Garden open: Wednesday through Monday 10:00 A.M. to 5:00 P.M. from April through October; weekends only during November, December, and March; closed January, February, Thanksgiving, and Christmas Day.

Further information: At the entrance don't miss the farm stand selling estate-grown apples and berries to help support the restoration. You can also pick your own fruit in season.

Directions: Montgomery Place is located on the east bank of the Hudson in Annandale. From the Taconic State Parkway, take the Pine Plains/Red Hook exit for Route 199. Go west 10 miles on 199 through Red Hook, turn right onto Route 9G and left onto Annandale Road. Bear left again onto River Road to the entrance. From Interstate 87 (the New York State Thruway), cross the Hudson at the Kingston/Rhinecliff Bridge (exit 19). Turn left onto Route 9G, and follow the directions above.

17. Stonecrop Gardens

Route 301 and Dennytown Road, **Cold Spring,** NY;
(845) 265–2000; www.stonecrop.org

*A*NYONE WHO likes gardens should find Stonecrop Gardens inspiring. For rock garden enthusiasts, however, these gardens are a must. A steep hill off a rural road in Putnam County's rolling countryside leads to this enchanting spot. Here, in an unusually idyllic setting, are some of the most glorious alpine and water gardens anywhere.

The Stonecrop estate enjoys pastoral views over meadows to distant hills. The beautifully designed grounds include a French-style country house with adjoining stable and wood fences, an enclosed garden, potting sheds and greenhouses, ponds and a lake, stone walls, plus the gardens. A woodland garden, pond garden, grass garden, and perennial borders are among the many tasteful plantings. But what gives Stonecrop its special cachet are its incredible rock and water gardens and alpine collection.

You'll find rock gardens throughout the grounds—from the area next to the house, where the plantings are displayed in tidy beds and in greenhouses, to the magnificent stream and cliff rock gardens beyond. And it's likely that you won't meet more than a handful of other visitors; you may have the place almost to yourself.

Before embarking on your exploration of Stonecrop, stop at the office (located just inside the house) to pay the entrance fee and pick up a map and descriptive guide. You might start with the enclosed garden, accessible from a scenic deck on the side of the house (the panoramic view from here is spectacular). Within a high wooden fence is an English-style garden with square and triangular beds containing vegetables and old-fashioned flowers. You can walk around winding pathways to see espaliers of lindens, dwarf apples, and pears and a romantic grape arbor. Guarding the scene is an effigy of Gertrude Jekyll, the great English landscape designer, curiously made to look like a scarecrow.

A path leads to the greenhouses and raised glass-covered troughs for displaying alpines. The carefully labeled exhibits are of museum quality and include every imaginable variety, most shown in the tiniest of pots in neat rows. If you are interested in learning in detail about these plants or care to embellish your own rock garden, this is a perfect opportunity. (You might compare notes with one of the gardeners, who can often be found working diligently in this area.)

You'll see other examples of rock gardens in front of the house. Many are on raised beds supported by stone or limestone (tufa) walls; especially delightful are miniversions shown on rectangular and round "pedestals."

To reach the most spectacular site of all—the rock ledge and the stream garden that precedes it—walk west from the house. What you see here more dramatically than anywhere else at Stonecrop is the result of an imaginative partnership between nature and human ingenuity. In the 1980s the naturally rocky terrain was enhanced by the addition of yet more rocks, including giant boulders, on the ledge. A network of gently flowing streams and pools was created, emptying into a lake below (with the water recirculating through underground pipes), and thousands of plants—mostly alpines, grasses, dwarf conifers, and Mediterranean species—were carefully placed for color, texture, and pattern.

The visual effect of the streams gently moving through the delicate plantings, around the rounded rocks, and into the clear pools is magical. Best of all is the fact that you actually walk down the cliff garden, stepping onto rocks that form it; in so doing, you feel more like a participant than a passive observer. As with the rest of Stonecrop, everything here is beautifully maintained and the plants are all labeled, even the tiniest. You can wend your way on a path of stepping-stones at water's edge to a charming wood pavilion covered with wisteria and similar in design to the main house (although in a more Japanese vein); this is a good lookout from which to enjoy the view.

The network of paths continues: around the lake, across a rustic stone bridge (known as the Flintstone bridge), and down the hillside toward the woodland pond. This lower pond is surrounded by primroses and woodland plants; from it a path leads through a grove of bamboo. You can explore it all at will, consulting your map.

Before leaving Stonecrop, be sure to walk on a small path through the woodland garden: Azaleas, rhododendrons, and other shade-loving plants have been carefully placed to blend harmoniously with this natural habitat. Nearby is a pond surrounded by lilies and groupings of an exotic species with giant leaves (apparently the largest herbaceous plant recognized). You would hardly imagine that this delightful pond was once a swamp: It is now maintained by artificial streams at each end. This is yet another example of the care, work, and imagination that have made Stonecrop the rare site it is.

✿ **Admission:** Fee.

Garden open: Tuesday, Wednesday, Friday, and the first and third Saturday of the month from April through October.

Directions: Take the Taconic State Parkway and exit at Route 301. Go west for about 3 miles. The driveway for Stonecrop is a sharp right, directly opposite Dennytown Road (the sign for Stonecrop is very small and easy to miss).

18. Boscobel

Route 9D, **Garrison-on-Hudson,** NY; (845) 265-3638;
www.boscobel.org

*T*HE GARDEN AT BOSCOBEL—an elegant, historic estate high above the Hudson River—might be described as a garden with a view. What a lovely garden! And what a view! For those of our readers who are seeking an exquisite flower garden with a panoramic vista of the Hudson and its marshes and waterways, this is the spot to see. We were entranced by the combination of artistic perfection—for such is the arrangement of Boscobel's dainty gardens —and the wild and natural patterns of the river below.

Boscobel has a fine house in the federal style (which you may visit to see English and American antiques and paintings) set majestically on a wide expanse of sloping lawn. The house was built in 1806 by States Dyckman following a pattern of the great Robert Adam. The estate includes a series of gardens nearer the bluff overlooking the river. The grounds—some thirty acres—are varied and well worth walking through. There is a flourishing apple orchard (which actually helps support the restoration), fig trees, fine old white pines, and tubs of oleander lining the walkways. A charming orangerie is filled with fruit-bearing citrus trees and other delicate plants. There is a small pond, wildflowers, and old-fashioned beehives known as skeps. From almost every spot you may glimpse the great river below.

The garden high points for us were the herb, boxwood, rose, and English gardens—all delicate and beautifully planned. Here on a flat portion of the estate are the series of colorful and intimate settings for the planting seasons, such as tulips and daffodils of delicately different shadings in the springtime, and roses and petunias throughout the summer. A small fountain is at the center of the formal gardens; edges are bordered in geometric patterns with boxwood and interlocking pathways. Benches are placed for enjoying both plantings and the view below.

Although Boscobel is not unknown to tourists, it is generally not a crowded place, especially during the week. There are some of the trappings of success as at all restorations, but we found the site quite unspoiled and, in fact, a place for both aesthetic pleasure and quiet contemplation.

❀ **Admission:** Fee.

Garden open: Wednesday through Monday from April through December.

Directions: Boscobel is located on the east bank of the Hudson River. From New York take the Henry Hudson Parkway, which becomes the Saw Mill River Parkway, as far as the Bear Mountain Bridge. Do not cross the river but pick up Route 9D and go north toward Cold Spring. Boscobel's entrance is on your left just after Garrison.

19. Clermont State Historic Site

1 Clermont Avenue, **Germantown**, NY; (518) 537–4240; www.friendsofclermont.org

*I*F YOU'RE A ROMANTIC, you'll find Clermont as inviting as the most delectable of feasts would be to a gourmet. Walking through these magical grounds is a treat to your senses, as you savor its captivating views, gentle river breezes, and delicious garden fragrances.

Everything about this enchanting Hudson River villa breathes romanticism—from its idyllic setting just steps from the river to its venerable old trees and lilac bushes, stone walls, banks of lilies, and sweeping, undulating lawns. You will want to wander at your own pace and follow the grassy pathways that lead to yet more delights.

Clermont has a long history. For more than 200 years—and seven consecutive generations—it was the country estate of the Livingstons, a prominent New York family. Originally part of the Manor of Livingston, a 160,000-acre tract granted to Robert Livingston in the late seventeenth century, it was developed by his son, also known as Robert of Clermont. Around 1730 construction of his brick, Georgian-style house was begun; it was named Clermont, French for "clear mountain," a reference to its views of the Catskill Mountains across the river.

Among its distinguished occupants was yet another Robert Livingston (great-grandson of the original owner), who not only administered the first oath of office to George Washington in 1789, but also served in the Continental Congress and helped draw up the Declaration of Independence. During the Revolutionary War, Clermont was burned by the British, no doubt because of the family's support of independence, and Livingston started construction on an elaborate, French-inspired new mansion (again named Clermont). While in Paris as Jefferson's minister to France, he met Robert Fulton, an inventor fascinated with steam navigation. Together, they built a workable steamboat (popularly called, not surprisingly, the *Clermont*), which made its maiden voyage between New York and Albany in 1807. It was on this occasion that the steamboat first landed at the Clermont dock, where Livingston announced the engagement of his cousin to his great friend and partner, Robert Fulton.

The manor house underwent significant changes over the years; among these, a new French-style roof in the 1870s and a complete remodeling during the 1920s. In 1962 the Livingstons deeded their historic estate to the State of New York, and it was designated a National Historic Landmark in 1973.

For all of its illustrious history, you'll find Clermont surprisingly intimate and rarely crowded. To reach the estate you drive through a large area of woodlands (the 450-acre Clermont State Historic Park) toward the Hudson. When you arrive, you should pick up a brochure with historic and practical information. The now-white and classically elegant manor house can be visited by guided tour only, but you are free to wander through the garden on your own (although garden tours are offered) and linger as long as you like.

The exquisite grounds include three main gardens: the sunken spring garden, the walled garden, and the upper garden. As you stand next to the house, looking toward the river, you see below you the sunken spring garden, which includes groupings of magnificent lilac bushes surrounded by vast, rolling lawns and the picturesque remains of an old stone barn. This romantic image alone is worth a trip to Clermont, particularly in springtime. The subtle coloring of the lilacs—ranging from delicate lavender to the deepest purple is dreamy, as is their incredibly sweet scent. Winding steps lead to the main garden level, where a vintage stone wall and terra-cotta urns containing flowers grace the side of the house. Surrounding them are manicured, terraced boxwood hedges; a few bird statues; and beautifully maintained lawns.

A flagstone walk will take you to the walled garden, enclosed by a delicate iron gate. Within lies a rock garden created in the 1930s by Alice Delafield Clarkson Livingston. Inspired in part by the Florentine gardens she had admired, it also combines some of the ideas of the noted British landscape designer Gertrude Jekyll.

Through the gate you come to a wilderness garden of irises and lilies. In the center is a pond, a favorite design element of Jekyll's. (It seems that the garden carp that once lived here would routinely winter in the house, in the Livingstons' bathtub!)

If you keep walking up the hill, you'll come to the upper garden and greenhouse site. Once planted with vegetables, it is now a cutting garden. Here you'll see peonies that date from the early part of the twentieth century.

Plan on spending enough time to explore Clermont and experience it fully. You might even enjoy a picnic while admiring the many views. (Picnic tables are tastefully distributed on the lawns and under the trees.) What could be nicer on a bright, sunny day?

❁ **Admission:** Fee.

Garden open: The garden, visitor center, and historic house are open between April 15 and Labor Day, Wednesday through Saturday 11:00 A.M. to 5:00 P.M., Sunday noon to 5:00 P.M. From Labor Day to October 31, Wednesday through Sunday, noon to 5:00 P.M.

Further information: Telephone to confirm hours and to check on tours. Clermont offers special events, including the Clermont Croquet Tournament (on those beautiful lawns!), an Old-fashioned Family Fourth of July, and the Chancellor Livingston's Art Show.

Directions: Take the Taconic State Parkway to the Red Hook/Rhinebeck exit onto Route 199 west. Go through the village of Red Hook. Turn right onto Route 9G (north). Drive 6 miles to the entrance sign for Clermont.

20. Vanderbilt Mansion Gardens

Route 9, **Hyde Park**, NY; (845) 229-9115;
www.nps.gov/vama/home

*I*F YOU ARE A first-time visitor to the Vanderbilt estate in Hyde Park on the banks of the Hudson River, you will be astonished by its magnificence. From the forty-room mansion of the Gilded Age, to the vast panoramic sweep of the property and its grand river view, to the ancient and majestic trees—it is a breathtaking place. The beauty of the Hudson River region was an inspiration for landscape designers as well as painters and writers, and the landscape design of Hyde Park (the formal name of the Vanderbilt estate) is spectacular. In 1841 Andrew Jackson Downing said: "Hyde Park is justly celebrated as one of the finest specimens of the Romantic style of landscape gardening in America."

This is one of the premier tourist sites in the nation. High school students studying the railroad monopolies, "great house" enthusiasts, tourists from abroad, and Americana experts are very much in evidence among the gilt and glitter of the house and the well-trod paths of the 240-acre estate.

But you'll find few visitors in the large, extraordinary gardens (which you can see without fee or guide). Placed well away from the house, they are both charming and unexpected—a touch of Italian elegance come upon suddenly from a wooden path. You'll find delightful architectural design and open space interspersed with carefully planned flower beds, clinging vines, and statuary. Warm-toned brick loggias and arches give this vast formal set of gardens an inviting air. Though you may wonder at the gardens being so far from the house, you can only be grateful that their quiet charm has survived the crowds visiting the mansion.

The estate's history includes several previous owners. In 1764 Dr. John Bard inherited the property—through his wife—from the first owner of the patent, Peter Fauconnier. Bard's home was actually across the Albany Post Road (you will still see the sign for Bard's Lane), but he made a path toward the river and the spectacular view.

His son, Dr. Samuel Bard, took possession of the property in 1799 and spent twenty-five years there. His house was the first on the magnificent riverside site. He is thought to have planted the giant ginkgo tree on the south lawn of the mansion.

The next owner (in 1825) was Bard's medical partner, Dr. David Hosack, who was noted for his interest in gardens; he was the founder of the first botanical garden in the United States. Needless to say, when he moved to the property in 1799, he soon engaged a landscape designer. In addition to planting the splendid and exotic trees that you will see throughout the estate, André Parmentier, the Belgian designer, laid out the sweeping roads, bridges, and lawns, in the romantic, natural style then popular—and still so inviting today. (The trees are so grand and numerous that there is a book devoted entirely to the subject for sale at the estate.)

The Bard/Hosack house burned in 1840. From 1840 to 1895 a family named Langdon owned the property as a summer retreat. They built the first real mansion there and created the formal gardens. The only structures that survive from their time are those near the gardens: the Gardener's Cottage, the Potting Shed, and the Tool House. You will note the High Victorian flavor of those buildings on the edge of the gardens.

It was Frederick Vanderbilt, grandson of Cornelius and son of William Henry Vanderbilt—both the richest men in America— who purchased the estate in 1895. The property was to become a monument to wealth and privilege. The Langdon house was replaced with the palacelike mansion one visits today. (It is open by guided tour.) Vanderbilt added sixty-four more acres and several new buildings, including the sixteen-room Pavilion (where the family lived while the mansion was constructed) and several guesthouses for friends.

Vanderbilt, however, left the magnificent landscape design of his predecessors alone for the most part; the trees and lawns and river viewpoints were already majestic enough to suit his taste for the grand. New bridle paths added to the look and feel of an English country estate. His extensive properties on both sides of the Albany Post Road produced prize-winning flowers as well as livestock and vegetables.

The formal gardens were of particular interest to Vanderbilt; he had a degree in horticulture from Yale and a lifelong interest in growing flowers and in farming. He asked a series of landscape designers to add terraces to the gardens, a cherry allée, a rose garden, greenhouses, and many small classical statues. Five greenhouses and a staff of twelve gardeners kept the gardens going. The formal gardens we see today are a combination of those from the Langdon and the Vanderbilt eras. Vanderbilt died in 1938, and the property has been a National Historic Site since 1940. During World War II, with funding scarce, the gardens deteriorated and the statues crumbled. Not until 1974 did restoration begin. Reconstruction was undertaken, walls rebuilt, plantings restored. But the gardens are today maintained entirely by contribution and volunteer effort.

You will find the formal gardens to the south of the mansion at the end of a small, winding gravel path that parallels the river bank. The gardens are set in a series of large, flat terraces that descend into a hollow. There are short flights of steps between them. The first impression is of color—the warm terra-cotta tone of the brick walls and loggias, the delicate black wrought-iron curlicues, the brilliant tones of flowers, and green throughout. They are Italianate in style—formal, elegant, and spacious—a style based itself on Greek and Roman plans. A particularly appealing aspect of these gardens is that the tier arrangement allows a view of all parts of the gardens from above.

The highest terrace, adjacent to the Gardener's Cottage, is a charming gazebo with a wishing well constructed of the same warm redbrick and wood. Just below it is the first tier of the garden. Here there are two long lines of square redbrick columns ornamented with delicate ironwork. The rows of columns are imitated by an allée of cherry trees and contrasted with oddly patterned flower beds. (Some 8,000 annuals and 4,000 perennials bloom in these spacious and elegant tiers.)

Just below is the second terrace, featuring statuary and pediments and a delightful pool garden surrounded by geometrically patterned flower beds. Irises, peonies, daisies, and poppies were in bloom when we visited. A grapevine-covered pergola with classical statue forms the boundary of this tier, and gray-green ferns decorate the borders. Each tier has inviting benches for visitors; you will feel far from familiar civilization here.

The lowest level contains the rose garden, dating to 1910. Planted with 1,000 rosebushes in differently shaped beds, this tier has a fountain and Italianate loggia that are enchanting. You can get a particularly nice overview of this level from the tier above. These formal gardens are only formal in design; they seem surprisingly warm and inviting.

Visiting the Vanderbilt estate can provide every sort of garden experience in one visit: You will delight in the majestic views and sweeping grounds and splendid trees, and you will find the Italianate formal gardens as special as any we have seen.

❀ **Admission:** Grounds free. Mansion charges a fee.

Garden open: The mansion and gardens are open for tours April through November. Call for hours.

Further information: Guided tours of the gardens are available during summer months.

Directions: The Vanderbilt estate is located about 80 miles north of New York City on the east bank of the Hudson River. From the Taconic State Parkway, take Route 55 west onto Route 9 north for 6 miles. The entrance to the estate is on your left. From the west bank of the Hudson River, take the bridge at Kingston to Route 9.

21. Innisfree Garden

Tyrrel Road, **Millbrook**, NY; (845) 677–8000;
www.innisfreegarden.com

*T*HE ARTISTIC GARDENS of Innisfree, near Millbrook, New York, are well worth a foray into the countryside. Created in the 1920s to reflect the philosophy and aesthetic of Chinese gardens, they bring you to a very different world from that of most gardens in the Mid-Atlantic region. Experiencing Innisfree means taking an inspiring journey and exploring nature through ancient Chinese artistic tradition. In fact, a walk here is akin to finding a series of Chinese landscape paintings that are real and three-dimensional, and then strolling right into them.

Walter Beck, a painter, and his wife, Marion, spent twenty-five years creating these vast gardens. Their inspiration came primarily from the eighth-century Chinese scrolls of the poet and painter Wang Wei, in which scenes in nature are unfolded gradually. The basic design idea of Innisfree is that of a cup garden—a Chinese tradition dating back hundreds of years. The Chinese would set apart an object by framing it in such a way that it would be distinct from its surroundings. According to Lester Collins, the landscape architect involved with Innisfree for many years, "You build a picture of nature; you control the floor and the walls, and you bring the sky down." Walking through Innisfree is analogous to walking through an art gallery from one picture to the next—from a meadow, to a rock covered with moss, to a lotus pool—in each case concentrating on the element before you. As in the case of a work of art, each destination has been created carefully to affect the viewer's senses in a certain way. Nature has been tamed completely and, even though the terrain at Innisfree may look wild and free, nothing has been left to chance. The land has been cleared, and waterfalls, streams, and pools have been created. "In their gardens," says

Collins, "the Chinese express life and death and everything together—the pain and the wonder." The two main elements of Chinese gardens—mountains and rocks (yang) and water (yin)—are very important in this garden and provide the necessary counterpoint of life. Yin is passive, dark, and moist; yang is active, bright, and aggressive. According to the Chinese, a harmonious arrangement of mountains and water can give the viewer a spiritual experience of universal harmony. Water and rocks of all sizes and shapes are everywhere set amid soft foliage, shrubs, and trees. Flowers are not an important element in Chinese gardens, but here you will find delicate clematis growing on an arbor, primroses, forget-me-nots, water irises, and hydrangeas.

Innisfree is a garden for all seasons, since it emphasizes the architecture of its basic elements in harmony with one another. (Note, however, that it is open only May through October.) You can enjoy it under any weather conditions, as a great garden "is good aesthetically and has nothing to do with climate," according to Collins. In fact, on one visit we experienced torrential rains. But the downpours only echoed the usual sounds of the nearby streams and waterfalls, and the soft colors of the foliage were rendered the more vivid by the rain.

Before setting out on your gardenwalk, you can pick up a map near the parking lot. A network of paths will take you around the lake (you'll see a tantalizing little island of pines that can be explored) and up and down gently sloping hills. Chinese gardens are supposed to be miniatures of nature's way; here too you will walk past small evocations of mountains, streams, and forests, experiencing each sensation as a traveler might in the open countryside, or as a viewer who encounters an unfolding Chinese hand-scroll landscape painting. You'll come across a mist fountain, a rock garden waterfall, a curious stone foo dog statue, a hillside cave, a brick terrace (where you can rest and take in the view), fantastic rocks in the shapes of turtles and dragons, birdhouses and bat houses, water sculptures, and hemlock woods. Don't fail to look about you at distant views as well.

✿ **Admission:** Fee.

Garden open: May through October: Wednesday through Friday 10:00 A.M. to 4:00 P.M., Saturday and Sunday 11:00 A.M. to 5:00 P.M.

Directions: Take the Taconic State Parkway; exit at Poughkeepsie/Millbrook (Route 44) and go east on Route 44. Look for Tyrrel Road on your right. The entrance to Innisfree is from Tyrrel Road.

22. Kykuit

Route 9, **Pocantico Hills,** NY; (914) 631–9491; www.nationaltrust.org/national_trust_sites/kykuit

*W*HEN WE FIRST HEARD early in 1994 that Kykuit, the Westchester estate of the Rockefeller family, was going to open to the public for guided tours, we were as intrigued as everyone else. Aside from a natural curiosity to see one of the private homes of this mythic American family, we were particularly anxious to view firsthand the extraordinary art collection we had all heard about. Judging from the large number of tourists who have since visited (despite the fairly hefty entrance fee and two-hour tour that must be booked in advance), the interest in this extraordinary site continues. And with good reason.

Kykuit (the name means "lookout" in Dutch) is a grand early-twentieth-century American villa magnificently situated with sweeping views of the Hudson River. It includes the imposing (although not ostentatious) mansion complete with its impressive art collection and antiques and, of greatest interest to us, the spectacular gardens filled with first-rate sculpture.

On the tour you are told (in mostly anecdotal fashion and perhaps greater detail than necessary) about the genesis of the estate—surprisingly modest in its earliest version—and its evolution with succeeding generations of Rockefellers; about the lifestyle of the family and its impact on the configuration of the house; about the provenance of the many artworks and objects. As we savored the gardens, we felt special admiration for the landscape architect, William Welles Bosworth, a personal friend of John D. Rockefeller Jr., who designed them in the first place.

Bosworth's gardens are considered among the finest examples of American landscape design. He placed two formal gardens—now containing the wonderful sculpture collection—on each side of the house, so they could be enjoyed both from inside and outside and could command the most formidable Hudson River views: one, a rectangular enclosed garden including a stone walk, manicured lawn, and clipped hedges; the other, an elegant rose garden. Bosworth also designed a Japanese garden (unfortunately not open to the public) and discrete spaces for golf and tennis. Throughout the gardens he added an eclectic but harmonious mix of classical motifs—terraces, pergolas, pools, fountains, classical temples, and grottoes.

Subsequent planting schemes (some under the watchful eye of Abby Rockefeller, who was a dedicated gardener in her own right) have enriched the gardens: a brook garden, particularly enchanting in spring with its blooming dogwoods and azaleas, and additional ornamental plantings on sleek green slopes and elegant terraces.

But the most impressive addition to these spaces has been the superb collection of modern sculpture, acquired and placed by Nelson Rockefeller. After having given away much of his art to major museums, he left some seventy important and large outdoor sculptures here. As you wander around the lovely terraces and gardens, you can enjoy the works of such twentieth-century masters as Brancusi, Giacometti, Nadelman, Matisse, Lachaise, Moore, Calder, and Maillol. The sculptures have been carefully placed to enhance each piece as well as the surrounding ornamental gardens, lawns, or walls.

Most of the sculptures have been left exactly where Rockefeller placed them, even in such unlikely places as the golf course. The majority are situated in the formal gardens next to the house. In the enclosed garden surrounded by linden trees you can see Elie Nadelman's *Two Circus Women* (another version can be found at the New York State Theater at Lincoln Center), Gaston Lachaise's *Elevation*, and Aristide Maillol's *Chained Action: Torso of the Monument to Louis-Auguste Blanqui*, to name a few. Some works have been dramatically placed to accentuate their relationship to the stunning panorama: for instance, David Smith's *The Banquet* on the villa's west porch against a scenic backdrop of the Palisades, Henry Moore's *Knife Edge Two Piece* against the surrounding rolling hills, and Alexander Calder's *Large Spiny* overlooking the Hudson.

You will probably wish for more time to linger in these glorious sculpture gardens that combine the best in contemporary art and landscape design.

❀ **Admission:** Fee.

Garden open: By appointment only.

Further information: Tours begin at the Kykuit visitor center at Philipsburg Manor in Tarrytown (from where you will be taken by minivan to Kykuit).

Directions: Take I–87 (New York State Thruway) to exit 9, and go 2 miles north on Route 9, following signs for Philipsburg Manor.

23. The Donald M. Kendall Sculpture Gardens at PepsiCo

Anderson Hill Road, **Purchase,** NY; (914) 253–3000

*W*E HAVE NO HESITATION in inviting you to take this outing; it is truly one of our favorites both with and without children in tow. You may wonder how PepsiCo—so well known for its mainstream popular culture advertising—would find itself in a book about gardens. But you are in for a wonderful surprise. While there are many public gardens and corporate art collections in America, few are available to the public to enjoy with the scale, variety, and quality of the Donald M. Kendall Sculpture Gardens at PepsiCo.

A walking tour of these 112 acres (more a landscape than a garden in the traditional sense) will introduce you to some major works of sculpture, as well as to a shining example of how a corporation can enhance its surroundings with beautiful grounds. The former CEO of the company, Donald M. Kendall, conceived the idea and was active in having the gardens designed and in collecting the sculpture to provide "an environment that encourages creativity and reflects essential qualities of corporate success."

In 1970 Edward Durell Stone's massive building was opened on this former polo field. The building (which is not open to the public) is made up of seven square blocks that form three courtyard gardens around a central fountain. The architect's son laid out the surrounding acreage of rolling green terrain; there are fields, pathways, a lake, distinctive trees, flower gardens, fountains, and—everywhere you look—sculpture.

The gardens themselves were planned by the internationally known landscape designer Russell Page; they continue to be developed today by Francois Goffinet. Pieces of art are carefully placed in relation to their surroundings, so that each knoll or valley provides a gentle setting for its work of art. There are both formal gardens, where smaller pieces of sculpture are bordered by clipped hedges and precisely groomed plantings, and vast fields—where monumental examples of contemporary sculpture stand starkly against the horizon. There is a lake and well-tended woodland. And then there is the newest addition to the gardens: a spectacular iris garden. The park is so carefully designed and maintained that even the parking lots are concealed by plantings, and an army of gardeners seems always to be at work.

To begin your gardenwalk, leave your car in one of the hidden parking lots (to which discreet signs direct you). No appointment is necessary, but check the hours listed below. You will seldom find this vast place crowded. After parking, go to the visitor center, pick up a numbered map, and enter the Golden Path—a nice, winding walkway designed by Russell Page. It meanders through the entire acreage. (You may wander on your own if you prefer, or stay on the path and follow the map, which identifies works of art and garden areas.)

As you come to the first fork in the path, go to your right onto the Golden Path, along a woodsy area dotted with daffodils and other spring flowers, and later with pink and white azaleas; in summer, European foxgloves are sprinkled among the red maples. The first sculpture, just to the left of the path, is Alexander Calder's *Hats Off*, a giant work in orange-red metal, unmistakably Calder's. It is set against a backdrop of white fir and Colorado blue spruce, bringing its brilliant color vividly to life.

Also to the left of the path is Jean Dubuffet's painted black-and-white abstract work, *Kiosque Evide*. And a little farther along, also to your left, is a work by Arnaldo Pomodoro called *Grande Disco*, a variation on the form of a globe eaten away by some mysterious forces.

Leave the path and walk left toward the building entrance to see a work by David Smith. This piece, called *Cube Totem Seven and Six*, is set just in front of the trellis to the giant headquarters building, amid a charming grove of plane trees. On the terrace above you'll find works by two twentieth-century Italian masters. First, you'll see Marino Marini's signature *Horse and Rider*. Also on the terrace are two Alberto Giacometti statues: *Standing Woman I* and *II*, their tall thin figures sharply defined against the building's wall.

Back on the Golden Path is Auguste Rodin's *Eve*, perhaps the most traditional work on this walk, charmingly set among holly trees and shrubbery. Nearby, to the right, is an interesting work by Max Ernst, *Capricorn*. Don't miss this surrealistic group of figures with animal parts suggesting fish, a cow, and birds.

One of today's leading sculptors is represented next. In a kind of garden area to your left you'll find Kenneth Snelson's *Mozart II*. This is a giant aluminum construction of geometric shapes and wires, a most contemporary tribute to Mozart. The backdrop for this sculpture is a pair of ornamental banks of pink Japanese rhododendron, crimson barberry, and spirea, among other delicately toned shrubs.

Go back to the path and turn left at *Mozart II* near the building's walls. Here is a spectacular view of sweeping lawn and great trees. You'll also see George Segal's *Three People on Four Benches*, a characteristically superrealistic work that may remind you of PepsiCo's workers relaxing during their lunch-hour break. Nearby is Claes Oldenburg's *Giant Trowel II*, one of the most memorable sights at PepsiCo (and one that garden lovers can easily relate to). In fact, it is so startling against its background of pine and dogwood trees that you blink to see if the giant spade is really there, digging into the green earth.

Moving farther along the path you'll next see George Rickey's *Double L Eccentric Gyratory II*, a typical Rickey work made up of stainless-steel windmill-like blades that shift gently in the breeze. From here you can see a graceful stand of thirteen different types of white birches gathered from around the world and planted in patterns. In contrast are blue grape hyacinths in spring and golden conifers year-round.

On the edge of the cultivated lawn, and in front of a wooded section, you'll come to Tony Smith's abstract *Duck* and Richard Erdman's *Passage*. Nearby you'll find the newest and most glorious of PepsiCo's garden innovations. In a woodsy setting crisscrossed by streams and small bridges is the new Iris Garden. Here, more than one hundred species of this glamorous flower have been imported from Japan and planted in undulating patterns among the trees. This is a sight not to be missed in late May.

Walk toward the building past the Oak Grove. Across the road you'll find the dwarf tea crab apples blooming in glorious pink during April. You will next pass the Franklin tree, one of the world's rarest specimens, discovered in 1765 by John Bartram (see the Bartram gardenwalk in the Pennsylvania chapter). This unusual tree is at its peak in August, when it appears in full white bloom. The Ornamental Grass Garden is next, a fascinating composition of different textures and colors.

You will now wish to see the courtyard garden, charmingly landscaped collections of plants and art. These are in the center of the building complex. Most artworks here are representative of the earlier schools of twentieth-century sculpture, including two Henry Moores, two Henri Laurens, and an Aristide Maillol. There is also a Seymour Lipton work and a David Wynne, *Girl with a Dolphin*, in the center of a fountain. Of particular note are the wonderful heavy figures of Laurens, *Le Matin* and *Les Ondines*. At the center of one of these sunken gardens you'll see an unusual Japanese star magnolia. Don't miss the pool, where you may walk on stone slabs through a watery environment that heightens your appreciation for the art so beautifully placed.

Exit the courtyard and go left, proceeding up a slight incline. On the terrace is *Personnage*, a 1970 work by the "old" master, Joan Miró, above the lily pond. This delightful garden spot, designed by Russell Page, has a perennial flower border and water lily pool. Here also is a charming gazebo inspired by the eighteenth-century English landscape design of Humphry Repton—a perfect place for a quick rest. A series of rectangular pools connected with stone slabs and grassy areas, this site is characterized by flowers and shrubs planted in pleasingly asymmetrical patterns. The overall effect is one of tranquillity. Brightly colored goldfish swim among the water lilies. Above is a hillside filled with rosebushes and flowering shrubs and Japanese cherry trees.

Next you'll come to one of the most memorable and defining works in the sculpture park: Arnaldo Pomodoro's *Triad*, a dramatic group of three modern, but ancient-looking, columns set starkly against the grassy landscape.

As you walk across the vast lawn, you'll come across several major sculptures and the entrance to the Azalea Garden. These brilliantly colored shrubs are at their best in May and June. Nearby are rare trees, including a lacebark pine from northern China and a European hornbeam.

The well-known British sculptor Barbara Hepworth is represented with a typical work, *Meridien*. Here also are the works of two noted sculptors who have defined contemporary sculpture in our time, in very different ways: Isamu Noguchi and Louise Nevelson. Noguchi's work, *Energy Void*, is a characteristically formalistic work framed with gray-green weeping hemlocks. Nevelson's *Celebration II* is a dark collection of geometric metal forms set in soft ground cover amid a stand of copper beech trees that reflect the color of the sculpture.

You have now reached the lake, bordered by graceful willows. In your walk around it you'll see several of the major works in the collection. First is Robert Davidson's three giant totems that will remind you of Northwest Coast Native American carvings. This work, appropriately called *Totems*, stands out by its audacity, bright colors, and dramatic design. Another contemporary work, Asmundur Sveinsson's *Through the Sound Barrier*, is also next to the circular path around the lake. And at the intersection of the lake path and your original entrance to the grounds is one of the most beloved sculptures (particularly by children), David Wynne's realistic *Grizzly*

Bear. The last work on the grounds is Henry Moore's *Double Oval,* which sits on the edge of the lake as a splendid monument to contemporary art.

Those of you who are interested in more detail concerning the rare plantings, including trees from all over the world, will find a list of these available at the visitor center.

The PepsiCo gardens are an unparalleled example of how in the twenty-first century a grand estate can combine vast landscape, formal gardens, and informal plantings with fine art.

❁ **Admission:** Free.

Garden open: Daily 10:00 A.M. to dusk.

Further information: The visitor center is open the same hours as the garden.

Directions: Take the Hutchinson River Parkway north to exit 28 (Lincoln Avenue). Follow the sign indicating SUNY/Purchase (which is directly across the street from PepsiCo). After you exit go left onto Lincoln Avenue and continue to its end. Turn right onto Anderson Hill Road; the entrance is on the right.

24. Lyndhurst

635 South Broadway, **Tarrytown**, NY; (914) 631–4481;
www.lyndhurst.org

*T*HE WORDS *grand* and *spacious* immediately come to mind in
describing Lyndhurst. As you enter the gates of this sixty-
seven-acre Hudson River villa, you drive through a parklike landscape dominated by broad lawns with giant specimen trees. Finally
you reach the mansion, considered to be one of America's finest
Gothic revival houses. Looming dramatically on the horizon, as in
a romantic novel, it commands sweeping views of the river. Around
it are majestic copper beeches, lindens, sycamores, chestnuts, and
maples.

It comes as quite a surprise to discover, in the midst of this
imposing setting, an unusually intimate and charming rose garden.
Rose fanciers will find it irresistible and alone worth the trip to
Lyndhurst, especially on a bright day in June. The garden is situated
in a grassy spot, away from the house and near the intriguing remains
of a once grand conservatory. Circular in design, the garden is built
around arched trellises surrounding a graceful Victorian gazebo. In
the midst are rosebushes and climbing roses in all shades of red, pink,
yellow, and white. Some are arranged in fanciful garlands. The roses
are deliciously fragrant—and profuse. Indeed, there are more than
one hundred varieties, some well over a century old. The rose garden was in fact created during the Victorian era, some fifty years
after the house.

Lyndhurst, originally known as Knoll, was built in the late
1830s for William Pauling, a former New York City mayor. It was
the first of a series of picturesque Hudson Valley estates designed by
Alexander Jackson Davis. Each of its subsequent owners added his
own imprint, especially railroad tycoon Jay Gould, its most famous
occupant.

Gould purchased Lyndhurst as a summer home in 1880. In addition to changing the house and gardens to suit his own taste, he decided to rebuild the greenhouse that had been destroyed by fire. He commissioned John William Walter, a designer of ecclesiastical architecture, to create an imposing Gothic-style conservatory in keeping with the aura of the mansion. Once the largest in the country, today it appears as a glassless and quite ghostly structure, awaiting further renovation.

It was Gould's daughter, Helen, who created the rose garden. (She took charge of the property after her father's death in 1892.) A source of joy to the Gould family and friends for years, it was unfortunately abandoned during World War II. But soon after Lyndhurst was bequeathed to the National Trust for Historic Preservation in 1961, the garden was fully restored to its former splendor. Today it is impeccably maintained by the Garden Club of nearby Irvington. No stray leaf or rose petal is to be found anywhere!

After you've seen the rose garden, you won't want to miss the Victorian fern garden near the entrance gate, also maintained through volunteer efforts; the Rose Cottage, a children's playhouse; and the Carriage House (its cafe features weekend lunches during the summer). If you are interested in learning more about the life of a bygone era in American history, you can take one of the regular guided tours of the mansion.

✿ **Admission:** Fee.

Garden open: Tuesday through Sunday 10:00 A.M. to 5:00 P.M. from May through October; weekends only from November through April.
Directions: From New York City, take the Henry Hudson Parkway north to Route 9 to Tarrytown; Lyndhurst will be on your left. From locations west of the Hudson River: take Interstate 87/287 and cross the Tappan Zee Bridge. Take the first exit (Route 9) and go south for about ½ mile, following the signs for Lyndhurst.

Don't Miss . . .

25. Storm King Art Center

Route 32, **Mountainville,** NY; (845) 534–3115; www.stormking.org

THIS IS A MAJOR art site (more than a garden site), but it should not be omitted from any list of important outdoor places where nature and art interact. Storm King is a must-see 112-acre landscape of rolling hills and spectacular contemporary sculpture; the startling contrasts between blossoming trees and towering modern art is unmatched anywhere we know of. There are semiformal gardens near the central building (set with David Smith sculptures) and rolling green hills dotted with flowering trees and shrubs amid the art.

❀ **Admission:** Fee.
Garden open: Wednesday through Monday from April through November. There are free walking tours at 2:00 P.M.

26. The Hammond Museum and Japanese Stroll Garden

Deveau Road, **North Salem,** NY; (914) 669–5033;
www.hammondmuseum.org

THIS INTIMATE Japanese garden is situated at the end of a rural road in the northeast corner of Westchester County. Befitting the idea of an Asian garden as oasis for contemplation, this site is about as silent and peaceful a place as you could find—except for the welcoming sounds of songbirds, crickets, even frogs. A small gravel path dotted with stepping-stones winds around a lotus pond and past groves of specimen trees, shrubs, and tiny individual gardens. With trail guide in hand (available at the entrance) you can identify katsura trees, bamboos, and Japanese varieties of flowering quince, larch, locust, cedar, smoke tree, among many others. Carefully placed rocks—some in the vertical position associated with Asian gardens—and stone statues of religious significance are scattered here and there: on a small island in the pond, by a flowering shrub, next to raked gravel gardens or the gently cascading miniature waterfall. You'll find garden benches along the way from which to contemplate it all.

We especially recommend visiting in late May and early June, for blooming azaleas, irises, and cherry trees, or in October, for vibrant fall foliage. A little outdoor cafe beneath a grove of planetrees serves a pleasant lunch during the summer months (call for reservations).

✿ **Admission:** Fee.

  Garden open: Wednesday through Saturday noon to 4:00 P.M. from May through October.

27. Springside Restoration

Academy Street, **Poughkeepsie,** NY; (845) 454-2060

SPRINGSIDE, a hilly, woodsy site once designated as an "ornamental farm" by Andrew Jackson Downing, is being restored by a hopeful, industrious group of volunteers. You may enjoy taking an authentic and detailed plan of its original state describing Downing's "landscape of the picturesque" in hand, and walking through the still overgrown grounds.

✿ **Admission:** Free.

  Garden open: Daily, or by appointment for a tour.

28. Untermyer Park

Route 9 at intersection of Odell Avenue, **Yonkers,** NY

THIS INTRIGUING PARK was once part of an elegant estate whose 113 acres were designed in a neoclassical tradition by William Welles Bosworth. Beautifully set high above the Hudson River, the park offers graceful plantings and classical antiquities galore, including a small temple, a grotto, Ionic columns, a Roman mosaic pool, and numerous ancient sculptures set among the flower beds, fine Japanese maples, and spectacular massive oaks.

✿ **Admission:** Free.
Garden open: Daily.

LONG ISLAND

29. LongHouse Reserve

133 Hands Creek Road, **East Hampton,** NY; (631) 329–3568;
www.longhouse.org

*L*IKE MANY GARDENS in history, those at the LongHouse Reserve in the eastern end of Long Island skillfully use the elements of surprise and illusion. But rather than employing traditional trompe l'oeil or playful waterworks that suddenly assault the unsuspecting passerby, this quintessentially contemporary environment provides surprise and illusion through an unexpected boldness of juxtapositions and combinations.

The LongHouse Reserve, creation of the noted textile designer Jack Lenor Larsen, includes sixteen acres of grounds with a remarkable glass and stone house inspired by a seventh-century Shinto shrine in Japan. Larsen, long fascinated by exotic icons from other cultures around the world (especially Asian, it would seem), incorporated many of these elements not only in his craft but also in the design of other objects and places—including this site. However,

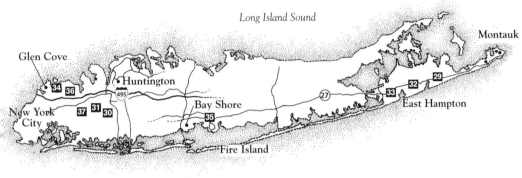

LONG ISLAND

29. East Hampton: LongHouse
    Reserve
30. Old Westbury: Old Westbury
    Gardens
31. Roslyn Harbor: Nassau County
    Museum of Art Sculpture
    Gardens
32. Sagaponack: Madoo, the
    Garden of Robert Dash
33. Southampton: David and Helga
    Dawn Rose Garden

Don't Miss . . .
34. Mill Neck: John P. Humes
    Japanese Stroll Garden
35. Oakdale: Bayard Cutting
    Arboretum
36. Oyster Bay: Planting Fields
    Arboretum
37. Roslyn Harbor: Cedarmere, the
    William Cullen Bryant Estate

there is nothing traditional about the house or its surrounding gardens.

LongHouse was built in the early 1990s as a showcase for contemporary lifestyle. In both house and garden, the emphasis seems to be on design for its own sake as an experimental art form, rather than as a complement to the surrounding natural environment. (The experiment is ongoing, since the garden, at least, is still evolving.) The imposing architecture of the house, with its overhanging eaves and stark, geometric forms, sits high on raised piers. Underneath is a huge outdoor living space leading to a patio. On one side, facing a rectangular reflecting pond, are crossed bargeboards atop high cement pillars, appearing to be futuristic windmills. Within the house are eighteen spaces individually conceived and designed by Larsen to display primitive and folk arts and crafts, as well as twentieth-century furniture.

The Asian theme of the house extends to a moon-viewing bridge that connects to the gardens. Larsen treated the outdoor spaces with the dramatic flair of a theatrical designer, obviously considering the relationship between artifice and nature. Near the house is a surprising group of man-made sand dunes topped with beach grasses. Apparently, during the excavation of the house and pond, huge amounts of soil were piled high. Larsen's imaginative way of concealing this inevitable eyesore was to have sand brought in by the truckload from nearby beaches. The sand covered the soil, and tall (but very decorative) dunes were born.

Throughout the gardens Larsen left his unmistakably strong design imprint. He contoured the otherwise flat landscape, fashioning artificial levels, berms, and pathways. The gardens are astonishing in their boldness of colors and materials. An extraordinary red garden includes an allée of cedar trunks painted a brilliant orange-red (much like the ceremonial torii gates of Japan) and surrounded by masses of red azaleas, Japanese maples, and flowering plums. At the end of the walkway is an imposing Japanese stoneware pot. (In fact, the gardens are an outdoor gallery for displaying arts and crafts as well as plants.)

Amid the grasses, bamboos, heathers, and seasonal plantings, you will find examples of contemporary sculpture as well as pottery and other artifacts. Some of the works are part of LongHouse's permanent collection, while others are on temporary display. Among the artists represented are Grace Knowlton, Jesus Bautista Moroles, Constantin Nivola, Toshiko Takaezu, Alfonso Ossorio, John McQueen, and Mary Frank.

The grounds include manicured woodlands with grassy trails, meadows, walled gardens, an impressive conifer collection, a laburnum walk, and two 1,000-foot hemlock hedges. There is a white garden with checkerboard plantings of boxwood and ilex alternating with white blossoms; a charming heather garden next to a long lap pool; and a sunken rose garden. (Roses are also paired with clematis, climbing onto long steel arches along a pathway.) In spring,

LongHouse has spectacular displays of daffodils along its winding paths. In fact, Larsen planted some 100,000 daffodils in 220 different varieties.

You will find walking through this unusual landscape (where garden equipment and machinery testify to its ongoing development) a rare experience, unlike any other in this otherwise flat stretch of Long Island. Both house and garden reflect Larsen's talent for creating new patterns and textures and his interest in generating public understanding of contemporary art and design. Long-House is open to the public on a limited basis for the time being, although plans are being made for more exposure. The various facilities include an outdoor acoustical amphitheater and indoor auditorium.

❄ **Admission:** Fee.
Garden open: Wednesday 2:00 to 5:00 P.M. during June, July, and August, as well as on occasional summer weekends.
Further information: An audio tour is provided with admission.
Directions: Take Interstate 495 (the Long Island Expressway) to William Floyd Parkway south to Route 27 east to East Hampton. From the center of town, make a left onto New Town Lane, continuing straight past the high school. Turn right onto Stephen Hands Path; make two sharp rights onto Cedar Street. Hands Creek Road is $^8/_{10}$ mile north of Cedar Street.

30. Old Westbury Gardens

710 Old Westbury Road, **Old Westbury,** NY; (516) 333–0048; www.oldwestburygardens.org

*T*HE MAGNIFICENT black iron gates and the grand allée beyond introduce you immediately to the glamorous ambience of Old Westbury Gardens. Here is the splendor of the magnificent European-style formal gardens of the past, their harmonious elegance graced with outdoor sculpture. This is a great estate on the grand scale, bringing to mind hazy romantic scenes involving Edwardian images and moonlit nights. In fact, the gardens are used frequently for movie sets and picture-book weddings.

Just a stone's throw from the ultimate contemporary highway landscape, this site is all the more intriguing in its contrast with Long Island sprawl. The estate, built in 1906 by John S. Phipps, a financier and sportsman, is not the only grand house in Old Westbury, where many of the rich and fashionable built their homes at the turn of the twentieth century. (Nearby are the William C. Whitney Racing Stables, for example.)

Phipps hired the London architect George Crawley to construct a Stuart-style "country" mansion to please his English wife. Westbury House was built atop a hill; its symmetrical elegance is set off by a master plan of landscape design. The estate itself is a rare example of landscape and architectural planning that went hand in hand; the complementary designs of the house and its surroundings are worth noting and are of great interest to modern designers and historians of landscape architecture.

The interior of the house is elegant and formal. It is open to the public and will appeal to those who enjoy seeing how such country retreats were designed and furnished—from fluted Corinthian columns and French windows to polished antique tables and ormolu clocks. You will find paintings by John Singer Sargent, George Morland, Joshua Reynolds, and Henry Raeburn.

But of particular interest and delight to us were the gardens. Even without the many sculptures, they are a work of art in themselves. Designed by both Crawley and a French landscape architect named Jacques Gréber, the master plan called for a formal geometric arrangement of grand allées, softened by English romantic or picturesque gardens. The combination, based clearly on the layouts of the grounds of English stately homes, is an unqualified success.

Among its charms are a lake walk—yes, of course, there is a lake—leading to a Temple of Love, a boxwood garden, a garden with flowers of all the colors of the rainbow, a "ghost walk" of dark hemlock trees, and a walled garden where you can easily imagine—or enjoy—the most romantic of trysts. There are numerous rare and magnificent trees and plants, including many from the Orient. Nearly 300 species of trees flourish at Old Westbury Gardens. Depending on the timing of your visit, you may see profusions of rhododendrons, lilacs, roses, and too many other of nature's most beautiful flowers to list here.

Sprinkled liberally throughout these enchanting areas are neoclassical sculptures and columns and various other artworks that add to the ambience of European elegance. Ceres is sheltered in a pergola of wisteria, while a terra-cotta Diana the Huntress graces a curving colonnade within the boxwood garden. There are ornamental cherub fountains in pools of lotus and water lilies; a pair of bronze peacock statues with topiary tails; an elaborate shell mosaic in the style of Italian grotto decoration of the seventeenth century; a sundial topped with rampant lions; groups of nymphs and satyrs on the roofline of the house; lead eagles and stone vases on pediments, surrounded by lilacs; and a sculpture of the quasi-mythical athlete, Milo of Cortona, wresting a tree stump from the earth.

❀ **Admission:** Fee.

Garden open: Wednesday through Monday 10:00 A.M. to 5:00 P.M. from May through December. We suggest weekdays when the gardens are not crowded.

Further information: Pick up a guide and pamphlet at the mansion.

Directions: Take the Long Island Expressway (I–495) to exit 39S (Glen Cove Road). Continue east on the service road of the expressway 1²⁄₁₀ miles to Old Westbury Road, the first road on the right. Continue ¼ mile to the garden entrance on your left. (You can also reach the garden by Long Island Railroad to Westbury from Pennsylvania Station in New York, and then by taxi from the Westbury station.)

31. Nassau County Museum of Art Sculpture Gardens

Northern Boulevard, **Roslyn Harbor**, NY;
www.nassaumuseum.com/ncma

*T*HIS SURPRISING TREASURE in the suburban sprawl of Long Island is a delight both to garden enthusiasts and art lovers. Here you'll find spacious and charmingly landscaped grounds providing a setting for a distinguished collection of twentieth-century sculpture, as well as a formal garden complete with gazebo. In addition, the museum's outdoor display includes a fine garden devoted entirely to the sculpture of Aristide Maillol.

The museum, well worth a visit in its own right, occupies the former Henry Clay Frick mansion. Frick bought the property from the noted poet and preservationist William Cullen Bryant. (See the Cedarmere gardenwalk for another nearby Bryant site.) It was Frances Dixon Frick, his son's wife, who with distinguished landscape architect Marian Cruger Coffin, laid out the gardens. Their inspired design has lasted very well and is kept in pristine condition today. (It is now owned by Nassau County).

The 145-acre estate is atop a hill and is spacious and inviting for walkers. There are numerous fine trees, many found in a pinetum of hundreds of conifers from throughout the world. The woodsy walking paths and rolling fields are set with sculpture by such noted artists as Reuben Nakian, Fernando Botero, Marino Marini, Roy Lichtenstein, and Mark di Suvero. (A printed guide to the sculpture is available at the museum desk.) To one side of the building you'll find the sloping, evocative Maillol garden.

The formal garden is different both in style and sensibility, though it too contains contemporary sculpture set amid the natural beauty. While the sculpture park is rambling and the works of art almost incidental to their settings, the formal garden is a throwback to earlier aesthetic taste. (These contrasts add to our enjoyment of the outing.)

Bordered by low boxwood hedges that accent the geometric walkways, the formal garden is divided into specific areas. Each path leads to another sculptural setting. There are a fountain and two odd figures called *King and Queen* by Spanish artist Xavier Corbero set amid the flowers, and statues by Chaim Gross and Jose deCreeft are beautifully placed within the arrangement of the flower beds. A lacy dark green gazebo lies near the rose gardens and an ever-changing display of seasonal plantings.

This is an outing that might particularly interest families with children, for it offers an opportunity to introduce both artistic and natural interests in a most enjoyable setting.

❊ **Admission:** Fee for museum entry only.
Garden open: Tuesday through Sunday 11:00 A.M. to 5:00 P.M.
Further information: For full garden pleasure, we recommend visiting in spring or early summer. Tours are available by appointment.
Directions: Take the Long Island Expressway (I–495) to exit 39N (Glen Cove Road north). Go approximately 2 miles to Northern Boulevard (Route 25A), and turn left. At the second light, turn right into the museum entrance.

32. Madoo, the Garden of Robert Dash

618 Sagg Main Street, **Sagaponack,** NY; (516) 537–0802;
www.madoo.org

*M*ADOO IS THE quintessential artist's garden. It is a vibrant collection of colors and shapes, compositions and patterns. Robert Dash, an abstract expressionist painter, then a landscape realist, and now again an abstractionist, has created a garden that reflects his artistic interests and spontaneity in some forty intersecting and interrelated garden parts. Unlike many designers of great gardens, he believes in the irregular. The overall abundance and ever-changing whimsy of Madoo makes this an original—unlike any garden we have visited.

Madoo (which means "my dove" in Scottish dialect) is a garden without the usual rules. Plants are mixed together with an eye for design and color; pieces of decor—painted vases, a jauntily posed straw hat, or sudden pieces of brightly colored furniture—are deliberately placed like bits of still life. Blueberries and roses share one area. Another is surrounded by high boxwood hedges that enclose a channel for rainwater; nearby is a sod bench like that seen in medieval woodcuts. There is an arched Chinese bridge, a laburnum walk, and abundant privet pruned to resemble dancers. Each section of the garden can be seen as a fanciful outdoor room with its own decor and visual logic. But these separate rooms of the garden share boundaries with one another, and from certain vantage points the viewer can see many sections as part of a whole.

Set on almost two acres of windswept land on Long Island's south shore, Madoo is directly next door to a working farm. The contrast between the neighboring long, straight rows of crops and Dash's wildly irregular plantings adds to the visual delight.

When the artist bought the property in 1966, it contained only some eighteenth-century sheds and a 1740 barn. Since then, he has moved structures and built two studios and two houses; some of the buildings form a low compound creating a sheltered courtyard for part of the garden. Even the brown weather-beaten, shingled buildings become part of the riot of color; the woodwork is presently painted violet and chartreuse, apparently to complement the current colors in the garden.

Begun in 1967, Madoo has evolved over the years into a whimsical and luxurious fantasyland. For the past few years it has been open one day a week in season as a conservancy, but the artist's creative personality (and amiable presence on visiting days) make a visit here a far cry from touring the usual impersonal and formal conservancy garden.

When you arrive (and pay the rather steep price—but it helps keep the garden going), you are given a map of Madoo. It designates forty areas and tells you how to get from one to the next. There are playful walkways, steps, and bridges if you follow the plan thoroughly. (One such construction is described as "a stairway to absolutely nowhere.") The map's accompanying description gives some idea of the scope of the artist's range of horticultural interests—from mazes, bird-welcoming plants, and a High Renaissance "view-swiper" perspective path to a fifth-century quincunx bed mentioned by Cyrus the Great.

Many of the plantings were chosen to withstand the heavy gales of the seaside site. Among the numerous flowers to be seen are some three dozen varieties of primroses, rugosa roses, Ship's rose and several other exotic rose species, 'Silver Moon' clematis, and yellow lilies and mullein. Exotic trees and shrubs include wonderful ginkgo trees, sculpturally pruned lilac and false cypress, weeping English oak, taiga birch, native pawpaw, and pollarded willows twisted in the wind. Three small ponds support a variety of grasses and border plants as well as frogs and fishes.

But all is not neatly arranged or described. There is an overall feeling of playful disorder and jungly overgrowth in parts of the property that make a visit here a bit like touring a funhouse in garden form. One section even has mirrors. And the artist's constantly evolving designs make it certain that every visit will be different from the one before.

✿ **Admission:** Fee.

Garden open: Wednesday 1:00 to 5:00 P.M. only during summer months.

Further information: Children under six are not permitted, but we recommend the garden for older children.

Directions: Madoo is in Sagaponack not far from East Hampton on Long Island. Take the Long Island Expressway (I–495) to Exit 70 to Route 27 east (Montauk Highway). One mile east of the Bridgehampton Village Monument, turn right at the traffic light onto Sagg Main Street. Go 1 ³⁄₁₀ miles, to number 618; the entrance is on the right.

33. David and Helga Dawn Rose Garden

Southampton, NY; (631) 283–2834

THIS IS A private, prizewinning rose garden so glorious that you may wish to drive all the way out to the south shore of Long Island just to see it. (But you can easily combine a visit here with stops at several neighboring gardens.) Here, in sight of a tidal creek and tongues of blue water of Shinnecock Bay and the nearby Atlantic Ocean, is a spacious green garden that is lavishly and expertly garlanded with roses—more roses of more different colors, sizes, and species than you probably knew existed.

There are roses climbing on trees, growing on a pergola, decorating the house, clinging to looping chain garlands on the edges of the garden, in clumps and beds and edgings—everywhere. Their colors vary from the palest of pinks and creams to the most brilliant crimson and peach and luminous white. Their sizes range from the tiniest and most enchanting, to the largest and most lavish full-blown blooms. Hybrids and prizewinning examples of varieties from Sweden, England, and Germany are intermingled with more familiar American species. A fragrance garden for Helga Dawn is in front of the house, while there are also species without fragrance at all.

David Dawn began his rose garden on the island some thirty years ago. He became increasingly interested in roses and traveled widely to collect new varieties. The result is one of the most successful private gardens we have come across.

David Dawn is a genial and interesting host, and he may take you around the garden in his golf cart, identifying any and all roses for you. Visitors are very welcome; while we were there photographers from a magazine were taking pictures of the pergola, so covered with blooming roses that a walk through it was like passing through a tunnel of heady crimson and white and golden blossoms. We were told that the garden is fully in bloom from June through September, with one variety of rose replacing another when its season is past. If you like gardens with only one type of flower imaginatively and lavishly designed, don't miss this enchanting spot.

❀ **Admission:** Free.
Garden open: In summer by appointment.
Further information: You will find David and Helga Dawn informal and hospitable to visitors.
Directions: Southampton is on the south shore of Long Island. Take the Long Island Expressway (I–495) to the William Floyd Parkway south to Route 27 east (Montauk Highway). Take Route 27A into Southampton. The Dawns will direct you from there.

Don't Miss . . .

34. John P. Humes Japanese Stroll Garden
Dogwood Lane, **Mill Neck**, NY; (516) 676–4486

THIS IS A contemplative Zen garden including stones, plants (especially many stands of bamboo), a teahouse, and carefully designed empty spaces.

❀ **Admission:** Fee.
Garden open: April through October by appointment only. Tours and explanations available.

35. Bayard Cutting Arboretum

Route 27A (Montauk Highway), **Oakdale**, NY; (516) 581–1002;
www.bcarboretum.com

THE BAYARD CUTTING ARBORETUM is one of the nicest landscaped places to take a walk on all of Long Island. Its plans were
drawn up by the landscape architecture firm of Frederick Law Olmsted, beginning in 1887. This elegant former estate of some 690
acres has everything: wonderful waterside paths overlooking a picturesque inlet with many white swans and geese, marsh gardens,
azalea and rhododendron gardens, sweeping lawns, small flower
beds, and the most stupendous weeping beech tree we have ever
seen. (If you love tremendous trees, this spot should not be missed;
there are many other fine old specimen trees, and the collection is
considered the best on Long Island.) The grassy and woodsy acres
of the arboretum surround a grand old 1880s mansion, the home of
the Cutting family, who sure knew how to live! Although there are
a few formal planted areas in this arboretum, this is more a landscape
than a garden. But it is a landscape for all seasons, even in winter,
when it is especially beautiful. Numerous classes and events are
held here, and Hackschner State Park is next door.

❈ **Admission:** Fee.
Garden open: Year-round.

36. Planting Fields Arboretum

Planting Fields Road, **Oyster Bay,** NY; (516) 922–9200;
www.plantingfields.org

THIS SPLENDID and vast arboretum was designed by the noted
Olmsted Brothers in the early part of the twentieth century, and it
is a horticultural showplace not to be missed. Its elegant grounds
(once the private estate of the Coe family) include majestic beeches,

lindens, oaks, and magnolias, as well as unusual shrubs imported from Europe and Asia. Among its many offerings, you'll find a Synoptic Garden with plantings alphabetically arranged by botanical name.

A visit to the two magnificent conservatories will lift anyone's spirits on even the bleakest of wintry days. The first, the recently renovated Camellia Greenhouse, contains an outstanding collection under glass. Camellias in delicate shades of red and pink are set among a delightful array of lilies. While these flowers are at their peak in February, the main greenhouse features brilliant seasonal displays year-round. Its poinsettias in December are almost legendary. Other plantings include orchids, delphiniums, bromeliads, and Spanish moss. An ivy-covered arch graces a corner, adding an elegant Victorian touch.

❋ **Admission:** Fee.

Garden open: Daily 10:00 A.M. to 4:00 P.M. The grounds are open daily 9:00 A.M. to 5:00 P.M.

37. Cedarmere, the William Cullen Bryant Estate
225 Bryant Avenue, **Roslyn Harbor**, NY; (516) 571–8130

THIS ESTATE of the romantic poet, journalist, and antislavery crusader William Cullen Bryant (1794–1878) suggests a nature poet's sensibilities. Now listed on the National Register of Historic Places and just being renovated, the lovely seven-acre estate overlooking the water includes a large house, a boathouse, a duck house, a watermill (built by Bryant to provide his own power), great trees romantically reflected in the pond, a charming bridge, ducks, and restored flower gardens. Bryant was an avid horticulturalist; the restoration is in accordance with his own notes and photographs. As of this writing the scenery retains an overgrown and pleasingly romantic aura; it is to be hoped that the restoration does not neaten up the place too much.

✿ **Admission:** Fee.

Garden open: Saturday 10:00 A.M. to 4:45 P.M., Sunday 1:00 to 4:45 P.M., and by appointment during the week from April through September. Tours available.

UPSTATE NEW YORK

38. Martin Lee Berlinger's Clove Valley Gardens

High Falls, NY; (845) 687-7895

*T*HIS PRIVATE GARDEN is set in deep country, the Sawangunk Mountains in Ulster County. But the steep, wooded hillsides and startling rock formations are surprisingly close to civilization, so a visit here is within easy reach of urbanites seeking a serene and unusual garden site.

In fact, serenity is precisely what Berlinger's gardens are about. There are half a dozen different gardens here; they are primarily Asian in conception and design, and each garden room offers a contemplative setting visible from windows of his house. Berlinger combines an obvious delight in the natural landscape that surrounds his property with a deep response to the mystical meanings of Oriental gardens. Each of the settings, with its careful designs of delicate, symbolic plantings, raked stones, and running water, opens out through a wooden gate to the magnificent landscape beyond.

An enthusiastic and knowledgeable guide, Berlinger is a professional landscape designer who spends half of his time in Asia. With his Thai wife he has created an ambience—both indoors and out—that is a surprising mixture of East and West. His interest in Thai and Japanese design is evident throughout his large, rambling house (which he hospitably offers to show too) and most of his gardens. This is a private site—neither large nor particularly showy—that truly invites visitors. As the owner is continually working on new plans, this could undoubtedly be termed a "growing" garden.

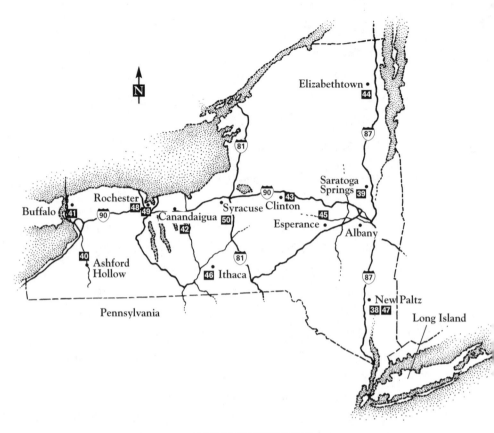

UPSTATE NEW YORK

38. High Falls: Martin Lee Berlinger's Clove Valley Gardens
39. Saratoga Springs: Petrified Sea Gardens

Don't Miss . . .

40. Ashford Hollow: Griffis Sculpture Park
41. Buffalo: Buffalo and Erie County Botanical Garden
42. Canandaigua: Sonnenberg Gardens

43. Clinton: Root Glen
44. Elizabethtown: Colonial Garden
45. Esperance: George Landis Arboretum
46. Ithaca: Cornell Plantations
47. New Paltz: Mohonk Mountain House Gardens
48. Rochester: George Eastman House
49. Rochester: Highland Park
50. Syracuse: Mills Memorial Rose Garden

In each garden room a different design has taken shape, but in all of them there is an attempt to capture something calming and orderly. These gardens are not dramatic statements; they are complete, small-scale environments that suggest tranquillity. You'll see the tall, exotic grasses (which deer do not care to eat), the asymmetrically shaped, stone-edged goldfish pond below the newly built pagoda (decorated with teak carvings carried back from Thailand), the delicate gates handmade from fallen trees and broom straws, the small statues of Asian deities hidden among the decorative shrubbery, and many stone benches for contemplative enjoyment. One garden, reachable through sliding doors from the bedroom, contains two stone islands, one symbolizing a tortoise, another a crane—representing wisdom and long life—floating in a sea of gravel. Each planting and positioning of stones has symbolic meaning. For example, the carefully pruned cedar tree suggests clouds, while the raked gravel represents waves.

But you need not understand the symbolic references to appreciate the design and ambience here. "I try to really change a space—its life, its feeling—because that will also change our lives as participants in that garden. Each garden creates different thought patterns, and each has its own effect on you," says Berlinger.

The Asian gardens are only part of the pleasure of visiting here. You will also see an English-style garden of great charm, filled with bulbs and perennials and—particularly in springtime—a profusion of color. Delicate pale green lamb's ears nestle next to brilliant yellow coreopsis, while red bee balm and scarlet crosomia 'Lucifer' are set off by white 'Casablanca' lilies and pale veronica. The English garden, though, also has a Thai touch: a statue of an Asian flute player perched amid the flowers.

At the edge of the cultivated gardens there is a pathway into the adjacent wooded area with its striking stony cliffs, which Berlinger has cleared of brush but left otherwise undisturbed in its natural glory. His seven acres abut a great forest preserve, with hiking trails throughout. A visit to this garden and its surroundings will suggest many new ideas to the amateur gardener—among them how to combine an appreciation for the natural wonders of a rural setting with carefully cultivated gardens of one's own.

❈ **Admission:** Free.

Garden open: By appointment.

Directions: High Falls is ten minutes from New Paltz, New York, at exit 18 on the New York State Thruway (I–87). Mr. Berlinger will provide directions to Clove Valley Gardens.

39. Petrified Sea Gardens

42 Petrified Sea Gardens Road, **Saratoga Springs**, NY; (518) 584–7102; www.petrifiedseagardens.org

*W*E'VE DESCRIBED many historic gardens, but how about one that predates history—one that is 500 million years old? The Petrified Sea Gardens will capture the imagination of anyone with an interest in geology, fossils, Native American culture, and—surprisingly—growing plants. Here, in a beautiful woodsy spot, you'll discover for yourself the huge and mysterious rock formations covered with fossilized "cabbages" that were once at the bottom of the Cambrian Sea. It is a rare and evocative—even cosmic—experience to walk on what was an ocean reef during the Ice Age, and to see the great cracks that seem to descend to the inside of the earth, and to touch with your fingers the fossil designs of growing things of an epoch beyond our imagining.

Surrounding these great slabs of stone are more modern areas: a few landscaped paths and a charming rock garden (of course!), a pond with goldfish and water lilies, and great trees. Designated a National Historic Landmark, the Petrified Sea Gardens retains a rustic charm; there are handmade signs with bits of information on them, and a little museum and fossil shop run on a shoestring by the family who owns the land (and by many volunteers). Open since 1993, the place has a nice lack of commercialism. There are no guides here; you make your way with a little map, and you can stay as long as you like examining this curious spot. We know of no other garden on the East Coast in which the modern plantings are so much less important than the rocks on which they grow!

Five hundred million years ago this area was at the edge of the Cambrian Sea; tides created great reefs, which were later polished by the glaciers into the smooth stone you see today. This fossilized reef is called a stromatolite reef because fossilized remains of single-cell blue-green algae (known as sea cabbages) and trilobite (sea bugs) cover the surface. The great crevices and small holes in the reef were the result of melting glaciers—some a mile thick—that wore down the rock face. (In 1923 a wandering cow fell and became stuck in such a crevice. During the cow's rescue, the fossilized reef was discovered.)

When you take this gardenwalk (on delicious red pine needle paths) as outlined by the map, you come first to a limestone grotto described as a place "where the earth can be seen to have slipped." Nearby along this forested path is the first section of the reef—truly an amazing sight. Though the area is quite flat, wear sensible shoes. Watch out for the many cracks and holes created a mere 12,000 to 15,000 years ago. Note the different sorts of crevices, holes, and scratch marks—described on the map.

Having traversed two great sections of the sea garden, you will come to what are known as glacial erratics: odd rocks and boulders carried along by glaciers and deposited here and there. To give you an idea of the glaciers' force, one of the three groups here weighs an estimated 200 tons.

We are not the first people to feel the cosmic force of these natural surroundings. This area is at the end of the Mohawk Trail.

The Iroquois Indians who inhabited the region thought of its glacial erratics in spiritual terms. The stones were oriented to the sun at solstice (one may have been used as an altar) and had great significance to tribes in the area. There is a circular stone dubbed the Medicine Wheel and a stone labyrinth. Also of importance to the Iroquois was

the great white pine, now 295 years old. Because it has five limbs reaching upward like a hand, it was called a Witness Tree; the Indians considered a vow made beneath it sacrosanct.

There are more familiar features at the Petrified Sea Gardens too: the rock garden—of a more contemporary nature—is very pretty, and there is a water lily pond complete with a small Buddha. You'll also find dinosaur footprints and a small museum of fossils. Bring the children! This is one garden in which they'll be thoroughly interested, and you too will find it intriguing to note that Mother Nature had her own unusually patterned "gardens" so long ago.

✺ **Admission:** Fee.

Garden open: Daily from May through October.

Further information: Petrified Sea Gardens offer tours and educational events as well as self-guiding maps.

Directions: Take the New York Thruway (I–87) past Albany to exit 13. Follow Route 9 north to Saratoga Springs; in town Route 9 becomes Broadway. At the intersection with Route 29 downtown, make a left and go west 3 miles to Petrified Sea Gardens Road; follow signs.

Don't Miss . . .

40. Griffis Sculpture Park

6902 Mill Valley Road, **Ashford Hollow**, NY; (716) 257–9344

THIS IS A vast sculpture park of about 400 acres of grassy hills, deep ravines, woodland, and open meadows—all set with a wide variety of contemporary sculpture.

✿ **Admission:** Free; donations accepted.
Garden open: Daily from April 1 to November 1. Tours by appointment.

41. Buffalo and Erie County Botanical Garden

South Park Avenue and McKinley Parkway, **Buffalo,** NY;
(716) 827–1584; www.buffalogardens.com

TWELVE GREENHOUSES provide more than two acres of gardens under glass—a special pleasure in winter in this harsh climate. There are outdoor gardens too.

✿ **Admission:** Free.
Garden open: Daily 9:00 A.M. to 4:00 P.M.

42. Sonnenberg Gardens

Gibson Street (Route 21), **Canandaigua,** NY; (585) 394–4922;
www.sonnenberg.org

THESE turn-of-the-twentieth-century gardens were designed by Ernest W. Bowditch of Boston. The Smithsonian Institution called the Sonnenberg "one of the most magnificent late Victorian gardens ever created in America." The splendid estate includes a conservatory, a rose garden, an Italian garden, lawns, ponds, and a belvedere. Later additions are a moonlight garden, rock garden, a pansy garden, a Japanese garden with a teahouse, and aviaries and a deer park.

The conservatory, built in 1903, contains an outstanding collection of tropical and desert plants.

❀ **Admission:** Fee.
Garden open: Daily 9:00 A.M. to 5:30 P.M. mid-May to mid-October.

43. Root Glen

107 College Hill Road, **Clinton**, NY; (315) 859–7193;
www.hamilton.edu

THIS LARGE wooded garden was created on lovely rolling terrain 150 years ago by Oren and Nancy Root. It features more than fifty species of trees and flowering shrubs, as well as peonies, irises, lilies, heathers, primroses, azaleas, daffodils, and raised beds of alpine plants. Visit in spring and early summer for best blooms.

❀ **Admission:** Free.
Garden open: Daily dawn to dusk by guided tour only.

44. Colonial Garden

Route 9, **Elizabethtown**, NY; (518) 873–6466;
www.adkhistorycenter.org

A WELL-LOVED, minute garden adjoining the Adirondack Center Museum re-creates elements of Britain's Hampton Court and Williamsburg's colonial restored gardens. This delightful retreat in a picturesque mountain setting has many colonial features: patterned brick and gravel walks, raised flower beds, a sundial, a 1776 cistern with dolphin fountain, iron benches, and a summerhouse surrounded by a traditional white picket fence. Flowers common to the eighteenth century include delphinium, heliotrope, phlox, dwarf cockscomb, columbine, foxglove, and cineraria; they bloom inside a border of cedar hedge. The garden is at its most beautiful in July and August, but its careful design makes it interesting even under a blanket of snow. A dense woodland adjoins the garden and is filled with wildflowers in season.

✿ **Admission:** Fee.
Garden open: Daily.

45. George Landis Arboretum

Lape Road (Route 20), **Esperance,** NY; (518) 875–6935;
www.landisarboretum.org

A NINETY-SEVEN-ACRE public garden, this Schoharie Valley arboretum is an ideal setting for long nature walks. The site features thirty acres of formal plantings, a twenty-acre woodland (where you'll see a white oak reportedly 500 years old), and numerous seasonal displays and programs concerning flowers, trees, birds, and other natural history topics.

✿ **Admission:** Free.
Garden open: Year-round; to see the flower gardens, visit from April 1 to November 15.

46. Cornell Plantations

100 Judd Falls Road, **Ithaca,** NY; (607) 255–2400;
www.plantations.cornell.edu

ON THESE 1,500 acres there are all kinds of gardens including a synoptic shrub garden; wildflower gardens; peony, herb, and azalea collections; and for those of you with a taste for something entirely different, a well-known poisonous plants garden. An arboretum designed by Olmsted protégé Nelson Wells and a conservatory of tropical and desert plants can also be seen here.

✿ **Admission:** Free.
Garden open: Daily dawn to dusk. Tours available.

47. Mohonk Mountain House Gardens

Route 299 west, **New Paltz,** NY; (845) 255–1000; www.mohonk.com

THE GIGANTIC nineteenth-century inn known as the Mohonk Mountain House is set in 7,500 acres of magnificent Catskill mountain scenery—including a lovely lake—whose beauty dwarfs any man-made flower beds or other additions to the natural panorama.

Mohonk has very pleasant formal gardens, as well as a fern trail and a wildflower trail. But you should not pay the stiff entrance price just to see these decorations to the sloping green at the back of the bustling resort. However, if you wish to enjoy (and pay for) the inn's many highly organized recreational facilities (including boating, golf, horseback riding, and miles of hiking trails), or if you wish to enjoy a copious meal at the inn, with its vast veranda overlooking the bright blue lake below (call in advance for a reservation), then visit the gardens while you're here.

We think you'll find the Victorian structures and the mammoth stone outcroppings that dominate the landscape of as much interest as the pretty rows of flowers (all labeled) and the hand-hewn wisteria arbors set amid the neatly cultivated lawns. A particular

pleasure to children is a tree house with a ladder almost completely obscured by vines. The gardens include a greenhouse that supplies the changing flowers seasonally, many gazebos, and several nice resting benches within these orderly beds, but not too much in the way of innovative design or exotic plantings. Nature's own extravagant beauties here are hard to compete with. Nevertheless, there is a formal rose garden, an herb garden, a show garden that dates from early days at Mohonk, a rockerie and pool garden, and wildflowers and fern trails.

Guidebooks to the arrangement of the gardens and the trails (including a "find it yourself" trail) are available at the gift shop within the main building.

You should know that a similarly glorious setting is nearby for free (or a nominal fee in summertime) at Lake Minnewaska, a park a few miles down the road. Here is a deep deep blue lake surrounded by huge cliffs of white stone that rivals any scenery we've come across. There was once a similar resort inn here, but no more. You can hike around the glacial lake or into the woods. And there are numerous other free hiking trails all along Route 299.

�֎ **Admission:** Fee except for guests.
Garden open: Year-round.

48. George Eastman House

900 East Avenue, **Rochester,** NY; (585) 271–3361; www.eastman.org

GEORGE EASTMAN, the father of popular photography, hired noted landscape architect Alling S. DeForest to create gardens all around the fine home—now a museum—on this twelve-and-a-half-acre estate. Today four beautiful flower gardens have been restored to their original elegance following Eastman's own photographs and the original plans. Among the pleasures are a rock garden with thirty-nine varieties of perennials in scalloped beds, a grape arbor, a pergola, a sunken oval water lily pond, seventeenth-century Venetian wellheads, a garden house, and more than ninety varieties of labeled perennials. There are many shrubs and vines and great trees.

❀ **Admission:** Fee.
Garden open: Tuesday through Saturday 10:00 A.M. to 4:30 P.M., Sunday 1:00 to 4:30 P.M.; open every day in May. Tours available.

49. Highland Park

180 Reservoir Avenue, **Rochester,** NY; (716) 244–7750; www.monroecounty.gov

THIS IS considered to be the best lilac collection in the world— there are some 500 varieties here! For best viewing come in late spring. There are also roses and a great conservatory collection of 40,000 plants on these exquisite grounds designed by Frederick Law Olmsted.

❀ **Admission:** Free.
Garden open: Daily until 11:00 P.M.; conservatory open daily 9:00 A.M. to 5:00 P.M.

50. Mills Memorial Rose Garden

Thornden Park, **Syracuse,** NY; www.syracuse.ny.us/parks/parks/thornden

YOU'LL FIND more than 10,000 roses, and lots of other perennials, blooming here in season. You can even visit this garden at night; it is illuminated!

❀ **Admission:** Free.
Garden open: Daily; come in June and July to see roses at their best.

Gardenwalks in Pennsylvania

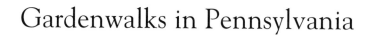lowers belong to Fairyland: the flowers and the birds and the butterflies are all that the world has kept of its golden age—the only perfectly beautiful things on earth. . . .

—OUIDA

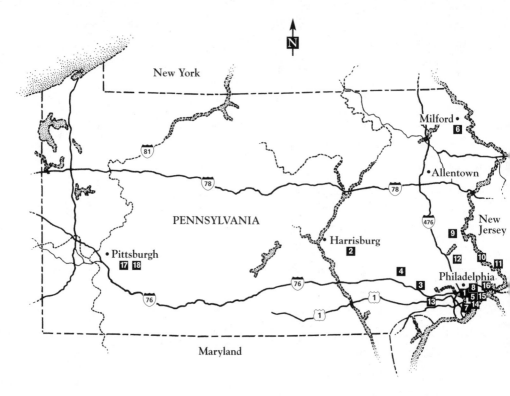

1. Gladwyne: The Henry
   Foundation for Botanical
   Research
2. Hershey: Hershey Gardens
3. Kennett Square: Longwood
   Gardens
4. Meadowbrook: Meadowbrook
   Farm
5. Merion Station: Barnes
   Foundation Arboretum
6. Milford: Grey Towers
7. Philadelphia: Bartram's Garden
8. Philadelphia: Morris
   Arboretum
9. Pipersville: Cedaridge Farm
10. Washington Crossing:
    Bowman's Hill State
    Wildflower Preserve

11. Wayne: Chanticleer

Don't Miss . . .

12. Chadds Ford: Brandywine
    Conservancy
13. Media: Tyler Arboretum
14. Philadelphia: Fairmount Park
    Horticultural Center
15. Philadelphia: Wyck
16. Pittsburgh: Phipps
    Conservatory
17. Pittsburgh: Pittsburgh Civic
    Garden Center
18. Villa Nova: Appleford

1. The Henry Foundation for Botanical Research

Route 23 and Henry Lane, **Gladwyne**, PA; (610) 525-2037

*W*HILE MOST of the rock gardens we have visited consist of small, delicate plantings set amid gentle, rocky slopes, the Henry Foundation gardens are something different. Here the rocks are giant boulders, dramatically punctuating the rolling hills. These striking outcroppings are massive hunks of Baltimore gneiss, and they give this garden a design all its own.

If you (and definitely your children) like climbing amidst rocks and flowers in a free-form environment, this is certainly a place to spend some time. The Henry Foundation gardens have used nature's amazing forms—including the unusually lovely, spacious terrain—to create a distinctive garden.

Finding this public garden is not easy. Even neighbors may not know of its existence. Set deep in the countryside of Philadelphia's Main Line, the garden is reached via some winding roads and a final dirt and gravel road that brings you to the entrance. But once you enter through the rustic gate (with a nearly illegible sign), you are in an enchanting—if eccentric—spot, like the proverbial Shangri-La. From the original mansion of the Henry family with its door wide open to the public, to the outbuildings that remind us of rural France, to the unbroken expanse of meadow and rock gardens, the Henry Foundation surprises with its charm.

The gardens date from the 1920s, when Mary Gibson Henry, a field botanist, began laying them out around the family home. She searched the American continent for more than forty years for plants that could survive in this rough and rocky terrain. By growing many unusual specimens at her Pennsylvania estate, Henry found that she had created a true research garden. The Foundation for Botanical Research—now forty acres—was created in 1948 to continue her work with rare and native plants.

The diversity of the landscape—from fields to steep slopes to rocky outgrowths to woodlands—has provided microclimates for plants with a great geographical range of origins. The plantings include warm-climate specimens from Texas and Florida and cold-climate examples from British Columbia and Nova Scotia. Depending upon the season, you'll see lilies and amaryllis in spring and amazingly colorful blooming Amaryllidaceae in winter. There are many flowering shrubs (such as rhododendron and snowbell), trillium, and bee balm.

The rock garden is spectacular, due both to the natural shape of the boulders on the hillside and to the plantings of gentians, yuccas, and silver bells, among other flowering plants. It is an energetic climb up to the boulders, but you have a great view once you reach the top.

Though you'll see the occasional identifying labels, this is not a uniformly tagged garden. There seems to be little organization—in the sense of a scientific, botanical center—but the planners' delight in color and design is evident throughout this unusual and comparatively unknown garden.

�֍ **Admission:** Free.

Garden open: Year-round, by appointment.

Further information: You might wish to time your visit not only by which season's flowers you prefer, but by when you would enjoy a rather hilly and rough walk. Unless you just wish to view the garden's delights from the driveway that runs through the middle of the estate, we recommend this gardenwalk only to those who are both energetic and good at climbing.

Directions: From the Pennsylvania Turnpike (Interstate 276), exit at Interstate 76 (Valley Forge). Go south on I–76. Take the Gladwyne exit and turn left. Turn right onto Route 23 and go for 2 miles. (From Route

476 in Philadelphia, you can take exit 6A to Route 23 east.) Route 23 is also called Conshohocken State Road. You'll find Henry Lane, a right-hand turn off of Route 23. After a short distance on Henry Lane, the road seems to end with a small park, but turn left and you'll see a private driveway and a small sign for the foundation.

2. Hershey Gardens

Hotel Road, **Hershey**, PA; (717) 534–3492; www.hersheygardens.org

*H*ERSHEY GARDENS are uncommonly pretty. Despite the surrounding atmosphere of the nearby Hershey amusement park, noted Hershey chocolate factory, tours, and hotels, these gardens are an oasis of pleasing landscape, bright-colored flower beds, very green mowed lawns, and amazing trees. The trees almost outshine the famous rose gardens. Not that the rose gardens are not magnificent. They are, and so are all the other flower beds and special landscape designs.

This is as much a landscape as a flower garden, with nice brick pathways through a rolling terrain, beautifully punctuated with gardens of all types and massive (labeled) trees. There are a pond and a fountain, brightly decorative annual and perennial beds, occasional statues and commemorative pieces, scattered benches and gazebos, and an extensive Japanese garden complete with boulders and stream. Your gardenwalk can take as long as you have time to spend, for each of the twenty-three acres has something of botanical interest. It is rather hilly; wear your walking shoes.

The gardens were developed over a fifty-nine-year period (beginning in 1937) from a three-acre plot of roses into a twenty-three-acre botanical garden and arboretum. Though originally planned at Milton S. Hershey's request (for a "nice garden of roses" to complement the community he had constructed for his workers), the years have seen a tremendous increase in sophisticated plantings.

In its original planting, 12,000 roses in 112 varieties were set out. The garden was an immediate success, drawing visitors from far beyond the town itself. By 1941 seventeen more acres of unused farmland were added and the gardens were soon displaying—in addition to roses—annuals, flowering bulbs, and the beginnings of a specimen tree collection, which is now so extraordinary. In the 1960s and '70s, dwarf and weeping conifers and flowering shrubs and many other beautiful trees were added. Today, under the operation of the Milton S. Hershey Foundation, the gardens are kept elegantly, and their flower displays are ever changing and brilliant in color.

We particularly appreciated the unpretentious, low-key, civilized atmosphere. There were few signs—though occasional plant labels—but we found helpful people at the desk, and a nice self-guiding map. Because of the many mowed lawns, a walk here is a bit like walking across a golf course with flowers.

Of major interest to most viewers is the rose garden, a sampler of dozens of species (these are all labeled) and planned to bloom throughout the growing season. Though rose gardens tend to be rather formal, these include an old-fashioned garden ("roses grandmother used to grow") as well as the original terraced Hershey Rose Garden. Colors range from the palest pink to salmon, lavender, and deepest crimson. Mermaid roses of pale yellow border the small lake, where swans and water birds and goldfish live. There are trellises of climbing roses, the orange 'Tropicana' rose, and a planting of the 'M. S. Hershey' rose, floribundas, grandifloras, tea roses, and miniatures. During the summer months (and often through October) some 30,000 roses bloom!

Your walk through the gardens will take you to other planted areas nestled among the specimen trees. You will see a rock garden, an ornamental grass garden, a plant doctor's trial garden, and, in spring, 600 brilliant azaleas and rhododendrons. The special display gardens change with the seasons: In spring 30,000 tulips and thousands of daffodils, hyacinths, and other bulbs bloom. Five thousand chrysanthemums appear in fall. The display gardens are laid out in patterns—a windmill design of tulips, for example, or geometric rows of similar color that resemble giant flags of flowers spread across the grounds.

All across the landscape are great trees, including varieties of ginkgoes ("nature's living fossils"), three California redwoods, incense cedars, bluish Atlantic cedars, a golden chain tree, and the extraordinary sinuous shapes of dwarf evergreens. There are maples and a giant weeping beech tree, poplars, elms, and dozens of other trees. As you stroll from garden to garden, these magnificent trees provide not only shade and interest but also a sense of wonder and permanence.

❀ **Admission:** Fee.

Garden open: Daily from April through October.

Further information: There is a yearly bloom schedule available, as well as daily tours.

Directions: Hershey Gardens are located 90 miles west of Philadelphia on Route 422 toward the town of Hershey. Follow signs to the hotel and the gardens.

3. Longwood Gardens

Route 1, **Kennett Square,** PA; (215) 388–1000; www.longwoodgardens.org

*T*HE LONGWOOD GARDENS hardly need an introduction. Among the finest of their kind in the east, they are a major tourist attraction year-round. And with good reason. The meticulously tended flower beds, topiaries, sunken gardens, grand allées, water gardens, and conservatories are a delight to all, young and not so young alike. There are 350 acres to explore, including an arboretum with ancient trees, a Victorian grotto, meadows of wildflowers, and forest lands. Walking through these beautiful grounds is a joy-ful experience; it is also easy and pleasant, and the terrain is flat and many paths paved. You can join a guided tour (Longwood is well organized in that respect) or pick up a walking guide at the visitor center and launch out on your own adventure. You will find you can easily lose the crowds as you wander through the many individual

gardens (eighteen in all), walk around the idyllic lake (com-plete with Grecian temple), or enjoy a picnic in the pastoral parkland.

Visitors are particularly drawn to the wonderful conser-vatories and the water gardens with their exceptional spec-tacles. Indeed, water gardens were the passion of Pierre S. du Pont, founder of Longwood and dedicated gardener in his own right. He had admired the ex-quisite water gardens in Europe and tried to duplicate them

here, adding touches of whimsy and elements of surprise that con-tinue to fascinate visitors.

A collection of fountains, canals, pools, basins, and moats graces the landscape, and the soft and appealing sounds of moving water are often heard. The Main Fountain Garden—a huge five-acre sunken area with rows of carefully trimmed maples surround-ing the waterways—features special water events: Water pours from the mouths of carved mythical creatures during five-minute intervals; 200 water jets shoot off water in fanlike shapes and arcs three times daily during the summer; and on summer evenings extravaganzas of fountains, lights, and music are held, much in the tradition of the French son et lumière (some say Longwood's shows are more spectacular). At the Open Air Theatre, a curtain of water completes the decor, and water displays occur regularly during and after dance performances.

Unlike Longwood's water gardens, the conservatories—seven in all on four acres—can be enjoyed at any time during the year, especially in winter, when their bright blossoms are most appreciated. The glass gardens include the Orangery (a charming 1920s crystal palace), the East Conservatory (undergoing restoration in 2005–06), and five interconnecting conservatories, including the azalea, camellia, rose, desert and palm greenhouses, some of which are also being renovated.

The conservatory complex includes an orchid house with changing displays, a Silver Garden, Cascade Garden, a collection of insect-eating plants, bunches of brilliant flowers hanging from baskets, topiary forms in large tubs, artistically arranged vegetable displays, and neat rows of nectarine trees.

Outside in spring you can enjoy the Flower Garden Walk with masses of lilacs, roses, tulips, irises, and peonies bordering each side of the brick path; the Rose Arbor; the Hillside Garden with its azaleas and bluebells; and the peony and wisteria gardens. The Topiary Garden, with sixty yews trimmed in curious geometric shapes, is always a popular spot.

The main house on the estate can also be visited. It's surprisingly modest considering it belonged to one of the country's wealthiest families. Many special events are held at Longwood Gardens, and you might wish to coordinate your visit accordingly: a November indoor and outdoor chrysanthemum festival; Christmas displays of poinsettias; indoor spring flower shows; band concerts, organ and choral recitals, and ballet performances; special programs for children; classes in horticulture and gardening for adults; and of course the famous water displays. There are even fireworks on special occasions during the summer.

The Longwood Gardens are indeed a year-round celebration of nature's joys.

✿ **Admission:** Fee for gardens; admission to the du Pont House is free.
Garden open: Daily 9:00 A.M. to 6:00 P.M. from April through October; daily 9:00 A.M. to 5:00 P.M. from November through March. Conservatories and shops are open daily 10:00 A.M. to 5:00 P.M. (or later when there are special events). The du Pont House is open daily 11:00 A.M. to 3:00 P.M. from April through December.
Further information: Facilities include a restaurant, cafeteria, and gift shop. Gardens, conservatories, and shops are all wheelchair accessible.
Directions: Longwood Gardens are located southwest of Philadelphia on Route 1, about 8 miles southwest of the intersection with Route 322. Follow the signs for Longwood Gardens.

4. Meadowbrook Farm

1633 Washington Lane, **Meadowbrook**, PA; (215) 887–5900;
www.meadowbrook-farm.com

*A*s YOU WIND your way along the quietly elegant tree-lined streets of Philadelphia's Main Line, you pass fieldstone houses set amid venerable old trees, generous lawns, and old-fashioned flower gardens. On one such street you might spot a discreet sign for Meadowbrook Farm, which could easily be overlooked by the casual passerby. This site includes several greenhouses and, of particular interest to us, the exquisite gardens of this private estate. These are a must on any gardener's itinerary.

Meadowbrook Farm was the lifework of horticulturist J. Liddon Pennock, who designed, created, and tended its remarkable gardens for almost sixty years. A descendant of a long and illustrious line of florists who first came to Philadelphia in the seventeenth century, he clearly was born with a green thumb. And an artistic eye.

The splendid thirty-acre property includes meadows and woods, the greenhouses and many colorful plantings around them, and his adjoining house with formal gardens.

The gardens occupy about one acre surrounding the elegant vintage stone structure. Combining intimacy with picturesque views, they are arranged in graceful sequence; one flows to the next, connected by brick walkways, allées, stone stairways, and terraces. Each is an individual room with focal points—among them an intriguing rotating fountain making graceful figure eights, a classical gazebo graced with Corinthian columns, and a pond with bright and lively goldfish. Water—in pools, ponds, and fountains—is a prevailing motif, true to the traditions of classic gardens. But these are not "water" gardens.

One thing that is most striking in the overall design is the combination of colors, shapes, and geometric patterns. The visual effects are formed by hedges in arabesques and rectangles, topiaries in varying types and sizes, and the always abundant flowers—jasmine, hibiscus, primrose, pansy, oleander. Complementing the plantings are graceful urns, small gray statues of animals and mythological themes, and well-placed benches from which to enjoy it all. Every inch of the gardens has been carefully planned, leaving not one bare, untended spot. They could have been designed by an interior decorator!

The greenhouses, from which many of the plants in the gardens are routinely taken, are worth a visit. This group of appealing conservatories is especially welcoming on cold, wintry days. Here you will find well-arranged displays of many different plants, some quite unusual. Outside you can wander around at will and enjoy more displays—extensive beds of annuals and perennials (hundreds of varieties), shrubs, and wonderful old trees.

Although the greenhouses are always open to the public, the private gardens are accessible on a limited basis—by reservation to small groups and only two days a year. But don't be put off: Try to make an appointment for your own private visit.

✿ **Admission:** Free.

Garden open: The commercial greenhouse is open Monday through Saturday year-round. The private gardens are open by guided tour only, by appointment, in May and October.

Directions: Take the Pennsylvania Turnpike (I–276) to exit 27 (Willow Grove) and go south on Route 611. Turn left onto Route 63 and go about 2 ½ miles. Turn right onto Washington Lane and continue for ½ mile. Meadowbrook Farm will be on your left.

5. Barnes Foundation Arboretum

300 North Latch's Lane, **Merion Station,** PA; (610) 667–0290; www.barnesfoundation.org/ed_a_main

*T*HE BARNES FOUNDATION ARBORETUM is distinctive for its connection to the internationally renowned Barnes Foundation, one of the richest—not to mention eclectic and eccentric—private art collections anywhere. The Barnes has long been an object of fascination. It consists of hundreds of paintings by some of the greatest masters, as well as thousands of valuable artifacts and objets d'art. The works are displayed in a decidedly unorthodox fashion: Crowded, sometimes four or five deep, they are mixed together without apparent consideration for style and period. Their bequest stipulated that they always remain as originally arranged. The fact that access to the collection has been—and continues to be—fairly limited has made it all the more intriguing to the outside world. As we write, its future in Merion Station is uncertain. (Be sure to telephone before visiting.)

The arboretum and the art gallery are parts of what was once the estate of Dr. Albert C. Barnes. This Philadelphia chemist, physician, and art connoisseur became a millionaire at age thirty-five from his invention of popular medicines. In the early 1900s he began to purchase paintings by contemporary artists who were yet to be widely recognized—particularly Renoir, Cézanne, Matisse, and Picasso. He also collected old masters and pieces of African art. The Barnes Foundation was established in 1922 to hold his remarkable collection and provide free art instruction to deserving students. The twelve-acre grounds (now the arboretum) surrounding the house were planted with diverse species and varieties of flowering plants to complement the art appreciation classes offered. To this day both the art gallery and arboretum are meant to further the educational and aesthetic benefits gained from studying art, trees, and flowers. Visitors view them together. (They are open at the same times and the admission fee includes both.)

While for most people the art gallery can be an overwhelming experience, the arboretum provides a pleasing and welcoming respite. Amid groves of lilacs (more than 250 varieties), rows of formal flower plantings, and many rare and mature tree specimens, you can contemplate nature's beauties—or the art you have just seen inside. Among the arboretum's many offerings are a formal rose garden with trellises and central fountain; an enclosed garden with stone walkways; a green-iron domed trellis graced with cascading wisteria; a woodland; and Mrs. Barnes's original greenhouse, where herbaceous plants are grown from seed. Most of the plants are carefully labeled (but you must know your Latin botanic terms).

✿ **Admission:** Fee.

Garden open: The arboretum and gallery are open at the same times: Thursday 12:30 to 5:00 P.M., Friday, Saturday, and Sunday 9:30 A.M. to 5:00 P.M.

Further information: Be prepared for possible lines; the Barnes Foundation is a popular destination.

Directions: From I–76 (the Schuylkill Expressway), take the Route 1/ City Avenue exit. Follow Route 1 south to Old Lancaster Road. Turn right and go about ²⁄₁₀ mile to North Latch's Lane. Turn left. You'll find the Barnes Foundation about ¹⁄₁₀ mile down the road, on the left.

6. Grey Towers

151 Grey Towers Drive, **Milford**, PA; (570) 296–9630;
www.fs.fed.us/na/gt

*F*EW GARDENS that we have seen have such an elaborate—or eccentric—architectural design as those that surround the medieval-style castle called Grey Towers. In a rural, off-the-beaten-track area of eastern Pennsylvania, you'll find this castle and its one hundred acres of grounds beautifully situated on a wooded hill beyond the small town of Milford (just a few miles from the much traveled Interstate 84). Like the mansion, the complex garden structures, walls, patios, pergolas, and the many outbuildings are all made of native bluestone, a picturesque and evocative material. The design of the entire estate creates a romantic sense of faraway times and places.

Grey Towers was constructed in 1886 by the Pinchot family, long residents of the area. The first Pinchot emigrated from France in 1816 (his charming house in Milford is now the Community House and public library.) James Pinchot was a prosperous manufacturer; his son, Gifford, was a noted environmentalist, appointed by President Teddy Roosevelt to head the U.S. Forest Service. Gifford Pinchot became governor of Pennsylvania in 1927 and lived at Grey Towers until his death in 1946. The site was designated a National Historic Landmark (with President Kennedy in attendance) in 1963. Pinchot's lifelong interest in conservation continues at Grey Towers today, where environmentalists still use the estate for conferences.

And what an estate it is! The forty-one-room mansion with its three great stone towers is in itself a cross between French medieval design (and furnishings) and affluent nineteenth-century taste. Its architect, Richard Morris Hunt (who designed the Metropolitan Museum, among other grand buildings) created an American castle curiously set just outside a thoroughly ungrand village. (The house is open for public tours in summer.)

Around the castle are many small buildings and the garden area. These constructions have such intriguing names as the Finger Bowl, the Baitbox, and the Letter Box, as well as the more familiar moat, ice house, and pergola. Pinchot's ideas for the grounds were the result of extensive travels—apparently both to foreign countries and into the past of his imagination.

Immediately beyond the dining room's French doors, for example, is the Finger Bowl, a raised pool surrounded by a mosaic terrace and tanks for aquatic plants. The "bowl" (a unique table with water in the center) was created after the Pinchots returned from the South Sea Islands. Here the family occasionally dined by candlelight, sitting round the pool's table edges and eating from Polynesian serving bowls that floated in the water.

Steps lead from this terrace to another enclosed stone-walled area (once the family's swimming pool) and now beautifully landscaped with wisteria vines and gardens. Surrounding the mansion are a complex set of gardens on different terraced levels—all of them created by the use of bluestone paths and walls and steps—as well as ancient-seeming pergolas and trellises. Many of the terraces contain gargoyles: Turkeys and eagles, among other beasts, appear in small niches and atop marble columns. And numerous statues decorate the place, including a bust of the Marquis de Lafayette in a niche on the second story of the house. There are vined gazebos, a rock garden, a water lily pond, benches, fountains, mosaics, a reflecting pool, and an amphitheater (used by the family for theatricals and campaign gatherings). At the far end of the reflecting pool is the Bait Box, built as a playhouse. Millstones taken from local gristmills also adorn the gardens. In among these many man-made divisions and artistic ornaments are luxuriant flowers and other plants. These are gardens in which very little of the design seems left to chance or to Mother Nature's own instincts.

All of these sites offer splendid views of the fields and wooded hillsides stretching into the distance. The trees—including a noted sugar maple planted by General Sherman more than a century ago—are notable. The vast wooded sections, including a spectacular and mysterious hemlock forest are today administered by the forest service. This is an inviting place for a walk.

A visit to Grey Towers might suggest a central question about gardens: Can the design created by architectural elements be overwhelming? Or are flowers and other plants at their most beautiful when organized by stone structures rather than by boxwood hedges or groves of shrubbery favored by so many landscapists? Grey Towers is perhaps the most architecturally designed garden we have seen, and as such is well worth a visit to this out-of-the-way spot.

❖ **Admission:** Free.

Garden open: Memorial Day to the end of September.

Further information: House and garden tours are conducted 10:00 A.M. to 4:00 P.M. daily, for a fee.

Directions: From I–84, turn south on Route 6 to Route 206 at Milford. Turn onto Old Owego Turnpike and follow signs. Grey Towers is on the left. Additional driving directions can be found on the Web site.

7. Bartram's Garden

Fifty-fourth Street and Lindbergh Boulevard, **Philadelphia,** PA; (215) 729–5281; www.bartramsgarden.org

*W*HILE MANY restored colonial gardens show us the orderly and useful aspects of early American gardening, John Bartram's extraordinary, less-than-orderly historic garden takes us on a flight of fancy. Located on the riverbanks of the Schuylkill on the outskirts of the city of Philadelphia, Bartram's Garden is a botanist's and historian's delight, as well as a pleasure to look at and wander through.

On this twenty-seven-acre hillside, just behind the 1730 house, are hundreds of tree and plant specimens that Bartram brought to the site more than 200 years ago—and that are still flourishing. The visitor gets a special sense of American history because the garden has been tended continuously and Bartram's design kept intact. Unlike many other colonial gardens, this pleasantly disordered place gives a sense of the excitement of settlers in a new world.

John Bartram was a Quaker Philadelphian who lived from 1699 to 1777. A farmer and botanist, he began the first thorough collection of native plants in this country. His garden was started in 1728 and increasingly became a passion as he gathered plants, seeds, and specimens of nature's bounty on the American continent. The adventurous botanist traveled all over the eastern half of the continent (as far as the Ohio River to the west and Appalachian Georgia and Florida to the south), carrying specimens back to Philadelphia in an airtight ox bladder. With his son, William, who continued the collection well into the nineteenth century, he established a commercial nursery, supplying seeds and plants by mail to such great gardens as Mount Vernon and Monticello. Bartram also received specimens from all over the colonies, from the West Indies, and from botanists worldwide. His carefully cataloged (and pictured) collection formed the first botanical garden in the country and included an astonishing 4,000 species.

The Bartrams also introduced some 200 varieties of American plants to Europe. Internationally known and admired, the father and son presented in England such subsequent staples of their world as mountain laurel and sugar maple. Frequently Bartram put together for shipment abroad "five guinea boxes" of the seeds of plants discovered on his travels.

When you visit the garden you will see—just behind the

house—his "common flower garden," his medicinal, vegetable, and herb gardens. But of particular interest is the fascinating collection of eighty-two different types of shrubs and trees about 400 yards down the gentle hill toward the river. Here you'll find giant oaks (known as Bartram oaks), and the famous Franklin tree from Florida, now extinct in the wild. There are ginkgo trees, prickly ash (whose bark was known for its toothache remedy), indigo bush, witch hazel, and bald cypress interplanted with mountain laurel, cucumber magnolia (brought from the shores of Lake Ontario), and the Fraser magnolia (from the Great Smoky Mountains). You'll see a pawpaw tree (of which legend has Bartram sending the fruit and flowers back to England in a bottle of rum), and in springtime masses of flowering dogwood, azalea, and wisteria. At the very bottom of the hill, you'll come upon old rocks and an evocative landing spot on the river.

Despite the occasionally weedy aspects of this garden—no doubt historically accurate!—you'll relish the sense of history and the mental image of the colonial Quakers arriving home from the American wilderness to plant ever more specimens of flowers and trees in their Philadelphia garden. If you find Bartram's Garden of interest, do not miss the collection of William's delicate and meticulous watercolors of plants or his interesting description of traveling and plant collecting published in 1791. Information on these historic items and even tours re-creating the Bartrams' journeys is available at the headquarters of Bartram's Garden.

❀ **Admission:** Free.

Garden open: Daily dawn to dusk.

Further information: Tours may be scheduled 9:00 A.M. to 5:00 P.M. daily. The house is also open to visitors; call for hours and fee. Picnics are allowed and lunches can be ordered in advance. The garden offers numerous educational and horticultural events. Note that the grounds are hilly and have occasional rough footing.

Directions: From Interstate 295 in New Jersey, take I–76 west (Schuylkill Expressway). After crossing the Walt Whitman Bridge, exit going west on Passyhunk Avenue. Turn north onto Lindbergh Boulevard; the entrance to Bartram's Garden is on your right at the corner of Fifty-fourth Street. From Interstate 95 in Philadelphia, take Island Avenue/291 west, turning right on Lindbergh Boulevard. Continue about 3 miles to the entrance, on your right, at Fifty-fourth Street.

8. Morris Arboretum

100 Northwestern Avenue, **Philadelphia**, PA; (215) 247–5777; www.business-services.upenn.edu/arboretum

*M*ORRIS ARBORETUM of the University of Pennsylvania is located well outside the city in a greenbelt. This is a lovely, hilly, Victorian-style park, filled with flowers and sculpture. Though the plantings and pathways are quintessentially Victorian and some of the loveliest we have seen, the sculpture is anything but old-fashioned. In fact, you might consider most of it totally unrelated to its surroundings.

The Morris Arboretum is at the site of a great house called Compton, which once belonged to a prominent Quaker couple named John and Lydia Morris. Though the house is gone, the 166 acres of landscaped grounds remain and are kept in most beautiful condition. This is a rather long and hilly gardenwalk if you want to see everything—and you should.

Originally designed by Charles Miller (an American of Anglophile tastes), the park is a marvel of charming paths, flowering shrubs, fountains, and clustered garden areas. There is a Temple of Love on a Swan Pond. There are numerous great trees—including twelve redwoods bordering a stream, a grove of cedars, the most magnificent flowering cherry tree we have ever seen, and many rare trees from the Orient. (You can pick up material about the arboretum, including a map and information on what's blooming, when you enter.)

There are many flower beds in the English style, as well as an indoor grotto with more than 500 types of tropical ferns. The rock garden, azalea meadow, and holly slope are worth seeing. In June don't miss the rose garden bordered by a wisteria allée. We could go on and on about the flowers and trees—but you will discover for yourself the natural beauties of Morris Arboretum. Be sure to plan your visit according to the season you most enjoy.

Now to the sculpture: The artworks are somewhat dwarfed by the beauties of the landscape. The Butcher Sculpture Garden contains predominantly contemporary art of which there are about a dozen permanently installed sculptures.

Several Cotswold sheep made of two-dimensional Cor-Ten steel by Charles Layland are "grazing" at the base of the magnolia slope. A kinetic steel sculpture by George Rickey called *Two Lines* moves in the wind. You'll see several constructivist pieces on the grounds, including Israel Hadany's *Three Tubes*, Buki Schwartz's *Four Cut Stones*, and a painted metal sculpture, *Untitled*, by George Sugarman. Linda Cunningham is represented by a giant bronze and steel sculpture that evokes the garden idea; its name is *Germination*.

At the center of the sculpture garden is a group of modern works by Scott Sherk based upon classical Greek mythology (but without classical visual connotations). Robert Engman is represented with a rotating geometric sculpture called *After B.K.S. Lyengar*. Thomas Sternal has made two wood sculptures from felled trees from the arboretum's own grounds; one is called *Table*, the other, *Altarpiece*.

The Morris collection also features several traditional pieces, including a *Mercury at Rest* (a copy of an antique sculpture excavated at Herculaneum) and some portrait sculptures of the Morrises themselves. Children will enjoy the Lorraine Vail whimsical animal characters, including a 5-foot frog and a bull.

The sculpture is widely separated by glorious patches of nature, which may give some viewers a sense of the art as a secondary source of decoration (as in Edwardian times). In fact, this type of massive contemporary art does not readily lend itself to such cultivated surroundings—except for young Mercury seated on a stone. Nonetheless, you shouldn't miss the experience of kinetic sculpture amidst the blossoms.

❀ **Admission:** Fee.

Garden open: Daily 10:00 A.M. to 4:00 P.M.

Further information: A map and plant information are available at the entrance.

Directions: From I–276 (the Pennsylvania Turnpike) take the Plymouth Meeting/Norristown exit to Route 611. Continue on Route 611 to Philadelphia, then take Stanton Avenue (right) northwest. The arboretum is between Stanton Avenue and Joshua Road on Northwestern Avenue.

9. Cedaridge Farm

Route 202, **Pipersville,** PA; (215) 766–2858

*T*HE RELATIONSHIP between art and gardens has surely been a long and mutually satisfactory one. Throughout history we find artists using nature's beauty as their inspiration and garden designers making nature into art. In this collection of gardenwalks you will find gardens that are closely identified with well-known art, whether as the subject of a famous painting, or as the re-creation of a landscape from a distant time or place.

No garden we have seen has made such a conscious (and successful) effort at reproducing an entire era of gardens—and paintings of them—as Derek Fell's Cedaridge Farm. Fell is a photographer and writer with a specialty in gardens and their history. His great interest is the French impressionist and postimpressionist landscape. Using reproductions of some of the most famous paintings made by such artists as Monet and van Gogh, he has created living versions of their subjects. At Cedaridge Farm you'll see bright-colored iris under a red arched Japanese-style bridge just as Monet pictured, and a perennial flower border around a vegetable garden, just as painted by Pissarro. There are fields of flowers as pictured by van Gogh, a leaf tunnel as described by Cézanne, and a jungle garden that captures Rousseau's oversize foliage.

A visit here is in fact a very odd experience. For the pure appreciator of pretty and well-designed gardens, it is a large, lovely, and ever-changing landscape. For the art lover who is familiar with the painting on which each garden tableau is based, it is beautiful but somewhat unnerving. It is like a visit to a famous portrait gallery in which each painted face has come to life.

This is a case of art imitating (and designing) nature and nature, in turn, being used to imitate art. We must remember that the impressionists planted their own gardens with paintings of them in mind. Monet, for example, chose and planted the flowers in his garden at Giverny because he liked their color harmonies, and he actually scattered seeds for tiny white flowers such as baby's breath across the landscape so that he could include their delicate touches in his paintings. Cézanne is known to have cut leaf tunnels through the flowering shrubs in his garden at Aix-en-Provence, giving it a sculptural outlook amid carefully harmonized greens. Renoir, another of Fell's inspirations, created a garden of wildflowers under the olive trees at his home near Nice, relishing the naturalistic look for his paintings. (All of these artists' gardens, by the way, are open to visitors in France.)

Using the impressionists' choice of plantings, color, and design, Fell has chosen to re-create a number of these sites. The flyer and map that you receive when you enter the property takes you from garden to garden. There is a nice, pleasantly informal atmosphere on this self-guided walk; nothing is commercialized or numbered on signs. You can see color reproductions of the paintings in the small house that is used as a gallery and headquarters for visitors. You may look first at the paintings and then see the gardens or, as we did, reverse the process. In any case, the verisimilitude is astounding, and we think you will relish following the map whether or not you are there merely to enjoy the pretty settings or are an impressionist painting enthusiast.

You begin your trail through an impressionist meadow of wildflowers and a rose arbor, which in turn will take you to a swamp garden. Next you will find your first garden inspired by a specific artist: Cézanne's Leaf Tunnel. This appealing spot is a study in light and shade, by means of close plantings of bright green Japanese hakone grass and sassafras, scarlet maples, and black walnut trees.

From here you will pass by water lily ponds and a stream garden, visit a Victorian-style conservatory, and enjoy a profusion of flowers in an old-fashioned cottage garden. Soon you will come to van Gogh's Cutting Garden, a brilliant re-creation of a scene the artist painted in Provence.

A gate designed and painted by Caillebotte (for a Paris garden) is nearby. A moon garden—one of our favorites—features a collection of flowers that are all white or pink so that they will reflect the light of a summer moon. From here you'll find a perennial-bordered, walled vegetable garden based on Pissarro's unusual design; it includes plants arranged both for color and shape, and a familiar wooden wheelbarrow and several watering cans artfully displayed. Nearby is a tableau featuring a rope swing like that painted by Renoir.

Le Douanier Rousseau's giant-leaved plants grow in a jungle-like setting at the bottom of a sloping hillside. These oversize plants include umbrella plant, joe-pye weed, plume poppy, and sunflowers. (This is a particularly exotic re-creation, since the artist's own paintings were imaginary rather than interpretations of the landscape. You might find yourself searching for a monkey or a lion amid the foliage.)

The Monet Bridge, with its delightful red arch, is surrounded by and contrasts with brilliant purple iris; it truly makes you feel you have wandered into Giverny by mistake. From here you come upon van Gogh's Woodland Garden, a grove of birch trees that forms a setting like that in his painting *Two Figures in a Landscape*. A visit to a moss garden and a ramble through the woods bring you back to the visitor center.

These are only a few highlights of Cedaridge Farm. The garden is apparently still being developed; perhaps when you visit there will be additional settings bringing to mind the shimmering colors and flickering light of the French impressionists and the shapes and forms that inspired the artists who followed them.

✺ **Admission:** Fee.

Garden open: Open to individuals only on Memorial Day weekend, Mother's Day weekend, and Father's Day weekend, Friday through Sunday 10:00 A.M. to 4:00 P.M. Open to groups by appointment on weekdays as well as weekends.

Further information: As this is a private garden, open weekends are subject to last-minute cancellation. Be sure to get a personal confirmation before you make the drive.

Directions: Cedaridge Farm is north of Doylestown in eastern Pennsylvania. You will receive specific directions when you make an appointment.

10. Bowman's Hill State Wildflower Preserve

Route 32, **Washington Crossing**, PA; www.bhwp.org

*A*s you walk along the woodsy trails and gentle creek in this lovely spot, you'll feel you are miles from the bustle of the highway and civilization. The preserve includes in its one hundred acres quite a variety of habitats—forest, meadows, ponds, bogs, an arboretum, and preserves for shrubs and flowers. An azalea trail leads to a path of bluebells; a marsh walk brings you to marsh marigold and holly areas; you pass the charming dam on the Pidcock Creek and come to the evergreen area. The more energetic can hike (or drive) to the famous Bowman's Hill Tower at the top of a surprisingly high hill in the preserve and thus complete their visit to this historic and lovely place. Your choices are extensive. This gardenwalk is hilly, but the preserve has more gentle trails as well. We recommend this outing to anyone who enjoys wildflowers, woods, and hiking. Children especially will enjoy the chance to roam freely.

Established to preserve Pennsylvania's native plants, Bowman's Hill opened in 1934. It is made up of twenty-six trails, including a trail for the handicapped (wheelchair accessible) and a famous arboretum called Penn's Woods, which has more than 450 different trees and shrubs. The general atmosphere of Bowman's Hill Preserve is relaxed. It is rather like wandering through a large, private nineteenth-century estate. There are few signs telling you what to do or not to do, and the fences and steps are made of natural materials that seem to have fallen naturally in place. The signs identifying the walks and plants are almost hidden by foliage and are never obtrusive, so you don't feel as if you are in a preserve but in a series of natural habitats. We found the preserve quite uninhabited in midsummer, but spring's profusion of wildflowers attracts more visitors. However, there is enough room for many walkers, and the trails are woodsy enough to absorb a fair number of people.

When you drive to Bowman's Hill Preserve, you will pass a picnic ground and public facilities near the entrance. Keep going and leave your car at the lot behind the headquarters. Pick up a guide to any of the trails and a tree and flower guide at the headquarters. You might want to bring your own plant identification books too. Insect repellent, stout shoes, and a picnic are all recommended. From here you can choose which of twenty-six trails you wish to follow, but most run into one another and you can't go wrong whichever you take. If you go downhill from the car park, you will come to the creek, which you can follow along its winding path. If you continue along the roadway (not accessible to cars) to its end, you will come to a rugged climb to Bowman's Hill Tower. If you go back in the direction of the entrance, you can walk through the arboretum. All of the trails should be seen, and the total walk is not beyond most walkers' endurance.

Among the arboretum's nine acres are familiar sugar maples, pitch pines, and American lindens, as well as the more rare chinquapin, cucumber magnolia, pawpaw, and black haw.

The hike up to the tower can be rigorous, and the trail takes you through dense underbrush. Your effort is well rewarded at the top. Bowman's Hill Tower stands on a hill 380 feet above sea level—one of the highest points along the Delaware River. The hill long served as a landmark, and before Washington's crossing of the Delaware it was used as a lookout and signal station. The present tower commands a view of 14 miles of the Delaware River Valley, including the very spot that Washington crossed. If you prefer to drive to the tower, you can get in your car and drive out of the preserve. Go back onto Route 32, turning to the right as you exit, and you will soon come to a sign to the tower. A winding drive brings you to a parking area at its base. The tower can be visited and climbed (every day but Tuesday) year-round. There is a small admission fee.

One of the most unusual and educational parts of this park is devoted to plants with medicinal uses, both real and legendary. The medicinal trail is a special walk for herb fanciers and those who are interested in natural cures or Native American herbal medicines. The medicinal trail includes plants of scientifically proven effectiveness as well as plants whose curative properties are nothing more than old wives' tales. A descriptive flyer tells you what you're seeing and what it's good for—or what legends say it's good for.

The trail, which is about 620 feet long, is slow going if you stop to examine each plant. While you are warned not to taste anything yourself—some of the plants are extremely poisonous—you are encouraged to go slowly and study each plant's story. *Note:* Due to the dangerous nature of many of the plants, this trail is not recommended for small children.

The trail begins with mountain laurel, the juices of which the Indians supposedly drank to commit suicide (although by 1800 a tincture made from its leaves was being used to treat several diseases). Next comes mayapple and bloodroot, a source of morphine that Indians chewed to cure a sore throat. Other plants include white oak, spicebush, wild ginger, alumroot, fairywand, and witch hazel. Among the old wives' varieties is ginseng, which Europeans thought restored youth (and which has been used for centuries as a cure-all in China). The list is a long one, and a walk along these plants is extremely interesting.

Other walks in Bowman's Hill Wildflower Preserve can of course be combined with this walk on the same day. There are a tree identification trail, wildflower trails, and several kinds of nature walks in this preserve. Several times during the year the preserve offers guided mushroom walks, bird walks, native plant and fern identification walks, as well as other wild plant walks. Each season brings different plants and appropriate events.

Admission: Free.

Garden open: Year-round except for major holidays.

Further information: Wildflowers are best in spring and early summer, but there is something to be seen in any season. One trail is wheelchair accessible.

Directions: From I–95 between Philadelphia and Trenton, exit for Route 32 and Yardley, Pennsylvania. Turn onto Route 32. Bowman's Hill Preserve is several miles northwest on Route 32.

11. Chanticleer

786 Church Road, **Wayne**, PA; (610) 687–4163;
www.chanticleergarden.org

*T*HE APPEALING LANDSCAPE of Philadelphia's Main Line is just right as a setting for natural-looking gardens. Many of the elegant houses are surrounded by gently rolling hills, deep green lawns, ponds, and stately trees—a perfect foil for all sorts of individual flower beds and garden design. Main Line estates like Chanticleer have room enough to spare; the flower gardens here are only part of an overall planned landscape.

Chanticleer opened to the public in 1993, and is under continuing garden renovation. It retains the feeling of a private domain, from its discreet entrance and its elegant lawns to the huge mansion with its walled gardens. Nonetheless, it is a pleasantly accessible place where you are allowed to wander as you wish, without a tour. The thirty acres of Chanticleer are enticing to explore, for they are often surprising in their plantings and design and are of both botanical and artistic interest.

When the Rosengarten family built the stately house in 1913, they chose the fashionable landscape designer Thomas Sears. (He also created the gardens at Appleford and many other private estates on the Main Line.) Sears decided to design formal gardens near to the house, so that one could step directly into them from indoors.

Thus, there is a courtyard garden that is unusually intimate. It has intriguing plants, including a rubber tree. By terracing the hillside just outside the library door on the east side of the house, Sears created the pleasure garden (are any flower gardens not for pleasure?)—a high Victorian concept that is beautifully adapted to this setting. It has a large slate terrace, formal walkways, stone walls, and elegant plantings. Surrounded by a hemlock hedge, the formal gardens include rose beds that are underplanted with rare plants and herbaceous borders. Viburnums, dogwoods, and other flowering trees make this a particularly pretty place in late spring.

This garden also has a view of uncommon beauty. Looking out over the expanse of sloping meadow, you can see the trellises of the brilliantly colored summer perennial garden far below, as well as a small pond and venerable trees. Walk down through the meadow (there is an agreeable absence of signs telling you where you may and may not go). In season you'll find wildflowers and native prairie plants throughout the meadow; this area complements the more formal sections of the estate. In April you may look back toward the house for an especially pretty sight: 50,000 daffodils in bloom.

Just beyond the meadow you'll find the newly created Asian Woods. Trees, shrubs, perennials, and vines native to Japan, China, and Korea are interspersed with great sycamores and maples. This will be a shade garden in which woodland plants—many rare in this part of the world—can be seen. You are encouraged to wander off the path.

From the Asian Woods you will come to the pond and stream, bordered with flowering herbs and ornamental grasses. On a still day the plantings are wonderfully reflected in the water. The path leads into a woodsy area of evergreens and tall Oriental spruce; May and June are the best times for seeing the woodland spring ephemera.

Farther along this path is the orchard, planted with forty flowering trees, including decorative crab apples of various colors. And

nearby are the English-style cutting garden, the flourishing vegetable gardens, and the summer perennial garden. The brilliant collection of flowers grows in wild profusion (especially recommended
in July and August). Both the flower gardens and the vegetable gardens are visual delights. Each area shows how an eye for design can
change the look of a garden: A wonderful espaliered border in dia-
mond patterns edges one flower garden, while the green of the vegetable gardens is dotted with giant brick red, terra-cotta urns.

A visit here can be educational as well as aesthetic; an identification list of the many rare and exotic plants is available on the
grounds. Chanticleer can be described as a botanical garden in a
country estate setting.

❀ **Admission:** Free; donation requested.
Garden open: Wednesday through Saturday 10:00 A.M. to 3:30 P.M.
from April through October.
Directions: From I–276 (the Pennsylvania Turnpike) take Interstate
476 south. Exit at Route 30 and head west. In the downtown of Wayne,
turn left onto Radnor Road, then turn right onto Conestoga Road.
Turn right onto Church Road.

Don't Miss . . .

12. Brandywine Conservancy

Route 1, **Chadds Ford,** PA; (610) 388–2700;
www.brandywineconservancy.org

NOTED FOR ITS conservancy of wildflowers, this museum southwest
of Philadelphia features the art of the Wyeth family. Its preserve
next to a busy highway includes five acres and a 1-mile nature trail
with year-round wildflowers. Pick up a map and listing at the
museum desk.

❀ **Admission:** Grounds are free; fee for museum.
Garden open: Daily.

13. Tyler Arboretum

515 Painter Road, **Media,** PA; (610) 566–5431;
www.tylerarboretum.org

THIS EXTENSIVE (650 acres) and inviting arboretum, one of the oldest and largest in the Northeast, is an ideal place for a long walk. You can enjoy miles and miles of beautiful, carefully marked paths and trails, where you will see impressive collections of shrubs and trees (some quite ancient and imposing) in the most natural of settings. A vast pinetum features spruces, pines, hemlocks, firs, and larches; groupings of flowering cherry, crab apple, holly, lilac, and magnolia brighten the ambience; specialty gardens surrounding a pretty stone granary include fragrant, butterfly, and bird gardens. Perhaps best of all are the historic so-called Painter trees, some twenty specimens well over one hundred years old. They are named after Jacob and Minshall Painter, two brothers who began the arboretum in 1825. Setting aside some of their land, the brothers went about planting more than 1,000 trees and shrubs in a most systematic fashion.

Among the arboretum's offerings today are classes, lectures, workshops, and other special events you might want to investigate. But we think the best way to enjoy these lovely grounds is to set out on a bright spring day, walking guide in hand (available at the visitor center) and soak up the atmosphere.

❁ **Admission:** Fee.

Garden open: Daily 8:00 A.M. to dusk.

14. Fairmount Park Horticultural Center

Horticulture Drive near Belmont Avenue, **Philadelphia,** PA;
(215) 878–5097; www.phila.gov/fairpark

FAIRMOUNT PARK is the largest city park system in the nation (and
in the world), and its 8,000 acres include 23 acres of fine garden displays, both indoors and out, many of seasonal interest. Of particular
note is the Japanese House and Garden, an authentic Monoyama-
style reconstruction (sixteenth and seventeenth century), complete
with golden carp pond, arched bridge, a bamboo grove, and native
and Asian plantings. There is also a set of demonstration gardens,
including Penn State's Accessible Garden, created by visually
impaired volunteers. It has raised beds, braille signs, and other innovations for the disabled, and it features ornamental and medicinal
herbs and many unusual flowers. There are numerous events held
in the greenhouse complex and outdoor areas.

❀ **Admission:** Fee.

Garden open: The horticulture areas are open Tuesday through Sunday 11:00 A.M. to 4:00 P.M. from May through August; weekends only
in September and October; and by appointment.

15. Wyck

6026 Germantown Avenue, **Philadelphia,** PA; (215) 848–1690;
www.wyck.org

WYCK is certainly one of Philadelphia's best-kept secrets. This historic colonial house and garden, in the heart of the once elegant
Germantown (now unfortunately a bit shabby), is not generally
known. The home of nine generations of a prominent Quaker family named Wistar, it even predated Independence Hall. Its collections of eighteenth- and nineteenth-century furniture, paintings
(including family portraits by Rembrandt Peale), ceramics, china,

and other objects accumulated over 300 years are a testament to its long history.

Wyck's enclosed grounds are intimate and delightfully old-fashioned. Outbuildings typical of traditional country properties—carriage house, smokehouse, and icehouse—are set amid flower beds and grassy expanses. But best of all is the rose garden. Its many (at least thirty-five, we are told) varieties of old roses are still arranged according to the original early-nineteenth-century design. This gracious garden includes circular walkways, a fountain, and gazebo.

To visit the house you must take a tour, but the garden can be seen either by guided tour or on your own. (In the latter case you must call first to check with the staff, since there is a watchdog on the premises!) Tours on architecture, decorative arts, garden history, and Quaker history are offered.

❁ **Admission:** Fee.

Garden open: For tours Tuesday, Thursday, and Saturday 1:00 to 4:00 P.M. from April 1 to December 15; or by appointment year-round. Phone ahead for information.

16. Phipps Conservatory

One Schenley Park, **Pittsburgh**, PA; (412) 622–6914; www.phipps.conservatory.org

THIS VICTORIAN GEM on a hill is the largest glasshouse conservatory in the nation. Each of the thirteen display rooms has a different type of planting. Among them are a palm court with marble statuary; a garden of topiary animals; and bonsai, desert plants, and orchid collections. There are changing exhibits as well.

❁ **Admission:** Fee.

Garden open: Tuesday through Sunday; closed on some holidays.

17. Pittsburgh Civic Garden Center

Mellon Park, 1059 Shady Avenue, **Pittsburgh,** PA; (412) 441–4442

MELLON PARK is a pretty, spacious, thirteen-acre city park in which a series of gardens have been created on the former grounds of a Mellon family estate. Though the house is now gone, the gardens have been maintained since the 1930s, and there are very nice antique-feeling touches here and there—stone steps and an occasional boulder or small statue, a sunken knot garden, a Shakespeare garden, an alpine garden, and even a model planting bed. This is a nice place for a walk among the shrubbery in spring or among the deep green, leafy trees on a hot summer day.

🌸 **Admission:** Free.

Garden open: Daily dawn to dusk. (And bring your dog; he'll have a lot of company.)

18. Appleford

770 Mount Moro Road, **Villa Nova,** PA; (610) 527-4280

THIS IS A twenty-two-acre preserved estate with a pretty, antique stone Pennsylvania farmhouse, duck ponds with waterfall, nice walks, venerable trees, and two small formal gardens that have a certain charm all their own. Created by the landscape designer Thomas Sears, Appleford's overall look is of natural hilly fields and a woodsy stream. But the high point for some garden enthusiasts is a low boxwood maze that will delight many little children (even if they can see over the tops of the complex design) as well as older visitors tagging along through its twists and turns. The formal rose garden is walled, decorated with statuary, and pleasingly intimate. The property is delectable in spring, with daffodils, rhododendrons, and lilacs in profusion.

❀ **Admission:** Free. Fee for house; tours required.
Garden open: Daily dawn to dusk.

Choosing an Outing

ARBORETUMS

Maryland
Salisbury State University
    Arboretum

New Jersey
Frelinghuysen Arboretum
Rutgers Gardens
Willowwood Arboretum

New York
Bayard Cutting Arboretum
George Landis Arboretum
Planting Fields Arboretum

Pennsylvania
Barnes Foundation Arboretum
Hershey Gardens
Morris Arboretum
Tyler Arboretum

ARTISTS' GARDENS

New York
Madoo, the Garden of
    Robert Dash
The Noguchi Museum
    and Sculpture Garden
    (Isamu Noguchi)

Pennsylvania
Cedaridge Farm
    (impressionist gardens)

ASIAN GARDENS

Maryland
Breezewood
Brookside Gardens

New Jersey
Sayen Gardens

New York
Martin Lee Berlinger's Clove
   Valley Gardens
Brooklyn Botanic Garden
The Hammond Museum and
   Japanese Stroll Garden
Innisfree Garden
John P. Humes Japanese
   Stroll Garden
The Noguchi Museum and
   Sculpture Garden
Snug Harbor (New York Chinese
   Scholar's garden)

Pennsylvania
Fairmount Park Horticultural
   Center

GARDENS THAT CHILDREN WILL ESPECIALLY ENJOY

Maryland
Ladew Topiary Gardens

New Jersey
Ringwood Manor

New York
The Donald M. Kendall Sculpture
   Gardens at PepsiCo
Petrified Sea Gardens
Storm King Art Center

Pennsylvania
Appleford
Henry Foundation for
   Botanical Research

COLONIAL- AND FEDERAL- PERIOD GARDENS

Delaware
The George Read II House
   and Garden

Maryland
William Paca Garden

New York
Colonial Garden
Mount Vernon Hotel Museum
   and Garden

Pennsylvania
Bartram's Garden

CONSERVATORIES AND BOTANIC GARDENS

Delaware
Rockwood Gardens

Maryland
Brookside Gardens
Cylburn Garden Center

New Jersey
Deep Cut Horticultural Center
Doris Duke Gardens
Frelinghuysen Arboretum
Skylands Botanical Garden

New York
Brooklyn Botanic Garden
Buffalo and Erie County
   Botanical Garden
Cornell Plantations
New York Botanical Garden
Queens Botanical Garden
Sonnenberg Gardens
Wave Hill

Pennsylvania
Bartram's Garden
Fairmount Park
   Horticultural Center
Henry Foundation for
   Botanical Research
Longwood Gardens
Phipps Conservatory

Pennsylvania
Appleford
Longwood Gardens

CONTEMPORARY GARDENS

New Jersey
Grounds for Sculpture
Sayen Gardens

New York
Battery Park City Esplanade
The Donald M. Kendall Sculpture
    Gardens at PepsiCo
LongHouse Reserve
Madoo, the Garden of
    Robert Dash
The Noguchi Museum and
    Sculpture Park

ESTATE AND FORMAL GARDENS

Delaware
Nemours Mansion and Gardens

Maryland
Hampton National Historic Site
William Paca Garden

New York
Boscobel
George Eastman House
Old Westbury Gardens
Sonnenberg Gardens
Vanderbilt Mansion Gardens
Wethersfield Garden

GARDENS LAID OUT OR INSPIRED BY FAMOUS LANDSCAPE DESIGNERS

Maryland
Hampton National Historical Site
    (Andrew Jackson Downing)

New York
The Donald M. Kendall Sculpture
    Gardens at PepsiCo (Russell
    Page and Francois Goffinet)
Fort Tryon Park (Frederick Law
    Olmsted and Calvert Vaux)
The Frick Gardens (Russell Page)
Montgomery Place (Andrew
    Jackson Downing)
Springside Restoration (Andrew
    Jackson Downing)

INFORMAL ENGLISH-STYLE GARDENS

Delaware
Rockwood Gardens
Winterthur

Maryland
London Town House and
    Garden

New Jersey
Cross Estate Gardens

New York
Clermont State Historic Site

ITALIANATE GARDENS

New Jersey
Georgian Court College

New York
Vanderbilt Mansion Gardens

GARDENS OF NOTABLE AMERICANS

Delaware
Nemours Mansion and Gardens
    (Alfred I. duPont)
Winterthur (Henry Francis
    du Pont)

New Jersey
Georgian Court College
(George Jay Gould)
Ringwood Manor (Hewitt family)

New York
Cedarmere (William Cullen
Bryant)
Clermont State Historic Site
(Livingston family)
George Eastman House
Kykuit (Rockefeller family)
Vanderbilt Mansion Gardens
(Vanderbilt family)

Pennsylvania
Bartram's Garden (John Bartram)
Longwood Gardens
(Pierre S. du Pont)

ORIGINAL AND ECCENTRIC GARDENS

Maryland
Ladew Topiary Gardens

New Jersey
Ringwood Manor

New York
LongHouse Reserve
Madoo, the Garden of
Robert Dash
Petrified Sea Gardens

Pennsylvania
Cedaridge Farm
Grey Towers

PALATIAL GARDENS

Delaware
Nemours Mansion and Gardens
Winterthur

New Jersey
Georgian Court College

New York
Kykuit
Old Westbury Gardens
Vanderbilt Mansion Gardens

Pennsylvania
Longwood Gardens

PRIVATE GARDENS

New York
David and Helga Dawn
Rose Garden
Madoo, the Garden of Robert Dash
Martin Lee Berlinger's
Clove Valley Gardens

Pennsylvania
Meadowbrook Farm

ROCK GARDENS

Maryland
Breezewood

New Jersey
Leonard J. Buck Garden

New York
Clermont State Historic Site
Stonecrop Gardens

Pennsylvania
Henry Foundation for
Botanical Research

ROMANTIC GARDENS

Maryland
Hampton National Historic Site

New Jersey
Cross Estate Gardens
Ringwood Manor

New York
Clermont State Historic Site
Lyndhurst
Montgomery Place
Wave Hill

Pennsylvania
Cedaridge Farm

ROSE GARDENS

New Jersey
Colonial Park
Deep Cut Horticultural Center
Lambertus C. Bobbink Memorial
　Rose Garden

New York
David and Helga Dawn Rose
　Garden
Lyndhurst
Mills Memorial Rose Garden

Pennsylvania
Hershey Gardens

GARDENS WITH
SCULPTURE

Maryland
Salisbury State University
　Arboretum

New Jersey
Georgian Court College
Grounds for Sculpture
Ringwood Manor

New York
Battery Park City Esplanade
The Donald M. Kendall Sculpture
　Gardens at PepsiCo
Griffis Sculpture Park
Kykuit
LongHouse Reserve

Nassau County Museum of Art
　Sculpture Gardens
The Noguchi Museum and
　Sculpture Garden
Old Westbury Gardens
Snug Harbor Cultural Center
Storm King Art Center
Wave Hill

SPECIALTY AND THEMATIC
GARDENS

Maryland
Lilypons Water Gardens
　(water lilies)
McCrillis Gardens (shade)
Sherwood Gardens (tulips)

New Jersey
Doris Duke Gardens
Frelinghuysen Arboretum
Rutgers Gardens (hollies and
　bamboos)
Sayen Gardens (daffodils)

New York
Brooklyn Botanical Garden
The Donald M. Kendall Sculpture
　Gardens at PepsiCo (irises)
Highland Park (lilacs)
New York Botanical Garden

TOPIARY GARDENS

Delaware
Nemours Mansion and Gardens

Maryland
Ladew Topiary Gardens
William Paca Garden

New York
Wethersfield Garden

Pennsylvania
Longwood Gardens

WALLED OR INTIMATE GARDENS

New Jersey
Cross Estate Garden

New York
Clermont State Historic Site
The Cloisters
The Frick Gardens

Pennsylvania
Wyck

GARDENS WITH WATER

Maryland
Brookside Gardens
Lilypons Water Gardens
London Town House and Garden
William Paca Garden

New Jersey
Waterford Gardens

New York
The Frick Gardens
Stonecrop
Wave Hill

Pennsylvania
Brandywine Conservancy
Longwood Gardens
Meadowbrook Farm

GARDENS WITH WATER VIEWS

Maryland
London Town House and Garden

New Jersey
Georgian Court College

New York
Battery Park City Esplanade
Bayard Cutting Arboretum
Boscobel
Clermont State Historic Site
Kykuit
Montgomery Place
Untermyer Park

WHEELCHAIR-ACCESSIBLE GARDENS

Delaware
The George Read II House
    and Garden
Winterthur

Maryland
Druid Hill Park Conservatory
Hampton National Historic Site

New Jersey
Colonial Park
Frelinghuysen Arboretum
Georgian Court College

New York
Bayard Cutting Arboretum
Brooklyn Botanic Garden
Central Park Conservatory
The Donald M. Kendall Sculpture
    Gardens at PepsiCo
Innisfree Garden
Lyndhurst
New York Botanical Garden
Old Westbury Garden
Wethersfield Garden

Pennsylvania
Longwood Gardens
Phipps Conservatory
Pittsburgh Civic Garden Center
Wyck

WILDFLOWER AND WOODLAND GARDENS

Delaware
Winterthur

Maryland
Cylburn Garden Center

New Jersey
Leonard J. Buck Garden
Sayen Gardens

Skylands Botanical Garden
Willowwood Arboretum

New York
Root Glen

Pennsylvania
Bowman's Hill State
    Wildflower Preserve
Brandywine Conservancy
Chanticleer

Garden Shows and Festivals

Delaware
Wilmington: Wilmington Annual
 Garden Day (May);
 (310) 652–1864
Winterthur: Azalea Festival
 (April); (800) 448–3883

Maryland
Annapolis: Bonsai Show at the
 William Paca Garden (May);
 (410) 263–5533
Baltimore: Daylily Society Show at
 Cylburn Garden Center (July);
 (301) 367–2217
Buckeystown: Annual Lotus Blos-
 som Festival at Lilypons Water
 Gardens (July);
 (310) 874–5503

New Jersey
Morristown: Annual Daffodil

Show at Frelinghuysen Arbor-
 etum (April); (973) 326–7600
Somerset: Annual Rose Daze at
 Colonial Park (June);
 (732) 873–2459. Also: Herb
 Day at Colonial Park (July)

New York
Brooklyn: Brooklyn Botanic
 Garden Indoor Bonsai Exhibit
 (January); (718) 622–4433.
 Also: Spring Bulb Show at
 Brooklyn Botanic Garden
 (February)
Buffalo: The Empire State Iris
 Society and Show at the Buf-
 falo and Erie County Botanical
 Garden (June); (716) 696–3555
Canandaigua: Rose Week at Son-
 nenberg Gardens (June);
 (716) 394–4922

New York City: The New York
Flower Show (March);
(212) 757–0915

Old Westbury: Rhododendron
Week (May) and Lilac Sunday
(May) at Old Westbury Gar-
dens; (516) 333–0048. Also:
Daylily Society Festival
(August)

Pennsylvania

Kennett Square: Easter Conservatory Display of Flowering Bulbs
at Longwood Gardens (March/
April); (610) 388–1000. Also:
Delaware Valley Daffodil Show
at Longwood Gardens (April)

Media: Holly Ramble at Tyler
Arboretum (December);
(215) 566–9134

Philadelphia: Philadelphia
Flower Show (March);
(215) 625–8250

Pittsburgh: Renaissance Faire at
Phipps Conservatory (August);
(412) 622–6914. Also: Fall
Flower Show at Phipps Conservatory (September/October)

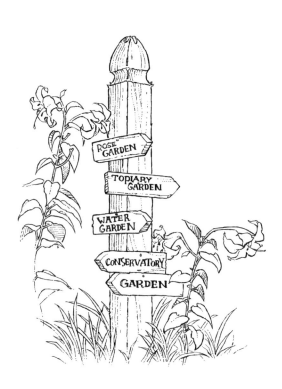

Glossary

allée: A stately tree-lined avenue.

arboretum: A place where an extensive variety of trees are cultivated for scientific, educational, or ornamental purposes.

belvedere: A structure such as a summerhouse situated to command a view.

bosquet: A small grove or thicket.

botanical garden: A place where a wide variety of plants are cultivated for scientific, educational, or ornamental purposes.

butterfly garden: A garden in which flowers are specially chosen to attract butterflies.

classical garden: A formal garden whose aesthetic attitudes and values are embodied in ancient Greek and Roman design.

colonial garden: A garden designed or reconstructed in the colonial American style, with separate sections for flowers, fruit trees, vegetables, herbs, and various outbuildings.

conservatory: A greenhouse in which plants are arranged for aesthetic display and in carefully controlled climatic conditions.

cottage garden: A small, unpretentious garden featuring flowers and vegetables in a casual arrangement.

cup garden: A garden in ancient Chinese tradition, in which an object is framed by its surroundings.

demonstration garden: A garden whose purpose is horticultural education.

English garden: A naturalistic garden style first developed in eighteenth-century England, as compared with the more formal French style.

espalier: A fruit tree or shrub trained to grow flat against a wall, often in a symmetrical pattern.

folly: A whimsical garden structure that is decorative rather than useful.

formal garden: A garden in which nature is trained to adhere to geometric or other formal decorative principles.

garden rooms: Individual, self-contained, and separately designed sections of a larger garden.

gazebo: A free-standing roofed structure, usually with open sides, that provides a shady resting place in a garden.

grotto: A small cave or cavern or an artificial structure made to resemble one.

ha-ha: A sunken hedge or moat that serves as a fence without impairing the view.

Italianate garden: A garden in the Italian style, often featuring classical elements, statuary, and fountains.

knot garden: Elaborate planting of greenery, usually thyme or box, following the patterns of knots.

maze: A garden labyrinth: an intricate, deliberately confusing, patterned network of hedges and pathways, designed to entertain.

naturalistic garden: A garden in which the design attempts to imitate nature in its free form rather than to impose form upon it.

orangerie: A sheltered place, such as a greenhouse, used particularly in a cold climate to grow oranges.

parterre: An ornamental flower garden whose beds and paths form a pattern.

pergola: An arbor or passageway with a roof or trellis on which climbing plants are trained to grow.

pleasure garden: A garden such as a flower garden or park, designed purely for enjoyment.

promenade: A place for strolling in a garden.

rock garden: A garden in which rocks and plants are arranged in a carefully designed, decorative scheme, often featuring alpine plants.

shade garden: A garden featuring plants that grow best in little or no sun.

topiary garden: A garden in which live trees and shrubs are clipped into fanciful shapes.

water garden: A garden in which ponds, streams, and other water elements, as well as plants that grow at water sites, are an integral part of the overall design.

wildflower garden: Usually a preserve, in which flowering plants grow in a natural, uncultivated state.

winter garden: A conservatory or other indoor garden that can be enjoyed all year.

Zen garden: A garden in the Japanese tradition, designed for beauty and contemplation.

Index of Gardens

A

Appleford (Villa Nova, PA), 215

B

Barnes Foundation Arboretum (Merion Station, PA), 192

Bartram's Garden (Philadelphia, PA), 196

Battery Park City Esplanade (New York, NY), 113

Bayard Cutting Arboretum (Oakdale, NY), 167

Boscobel (Garrison-on-Hudson, NY), 130

Bowman's Hill State Wildflower Preserve (Washington Crossing, PA), 205

Brandywine Conservancy (Chadds Ford, PA), 210

Breezewood (Monkton, MD), 57

Brooklyn Botanic Garden (Brooklyn, NY), 93

Brookside Gardens (Wheaton, MD), 53

Buffalo and Erie County Botanical Garden (Buffalo, NY), 175

C

Cedaridge Farm (Pipersville, PA), 201

Cedarmere, the William Cullen Bryant Estate (Roslyn Harbor, NY), 168

Central Park Conservancy Garden, The (New York, NY), 115

Chanticleer (Wayne, PA), 208

Clermont State Historic Site (Germantown, NY), 131

Cloisters, The (New York, NY), 106

Colonial Garden (Elizabethtown, NY), 176

Colonial Park (Somerset, NJ), 80

Cornell Plantations (Ithaca, NY), 177

Cross Estate Gardens (Bernardsville, NJ), 61

Cylburn Garden Center (Baltimore, MD), 55

D

David and Helga Dawn Rose Garden (Southampton, NY), 165

Deep Cut Park Horticultural Center (Middletown, NJ), 68

Donald M. Kendall Sculpture Gardens at PepsiCo, The (Purchase, NY), 143

Doris Duke Gardens (Somerville, NJ), 81

Druid Hill Park Conservatory (Baltimore, MD), 55

F

Fairmount Park Horticultural Center (Philadelphia, PA), 212

Ford Foundation Garden (New York, NY), 115

Fort Tryon Park (New York, NY), 116

Frelinghuysen Arboretum (Morristown, NJ), 71

Frick Gardens, The (New York, NY), 110

G

George Eastman House (Rochester, NY), 179

George Landis Arboretum (Esperance, NY), 177

George Read II House and Garden, The (New Castle, DE), 41

Georgian Court College (Lakewood, NJ), 66

Grey Towers (Milford, PA), 194

Griffis Sculpture Park (Ashford Hollow, NY), 175

Grounds for Sculpture (Hamilton, NJ), 86

H

Hagley Museum and Library (Wilmington, DE), 41

Hammond Museum and Japanese Stroll Garden, The (North Salem, NY), 152

Hampton National Historic Site (Towson, MD), 51

Henry Foundation for Botanical Research (Gladwyne, PA), 183

Hershey Gardens (Hershey, PA), 185

Highland Park (Rochester, NY), 180

I

Innisfree Garden (Millbrook, NY), 139

J

John P. Humes Japanese Stroll Garden (Mill Neck, NY), 166

K

Kykuit (Pocantico Hills, NY), 141

L

Ladew Topiary Gardens (Monkton, MD), 50

Lambertus C. Bobbink Memorial Rose Garden (Lincroft, NJ), 87

Leaming's Run Gardens (Swainton, NJ), 89

Leonard J. Buck Garden (Far Hills, NJ), 62

Lilypons Water Gardens (Buckeystown, MD), 57

London Town House and Garden (Edgewater, MD), 48

LongHouse Reserve (East Hampton, NY), 154

Longwood Gardens (Kennett Square, PA), 187

Lyndhurst (Tarrytown, NY), 150

Madoo, the Garden of Robert Dash (Sagaponack, NY), 162

Martin Lee Berlinger's Clove Valley Gardens (High Falls, NY), 169

McCrillis Gardens (Bethesda, MD), 56

Meadowbrook Farm (Meadowbrook, PA), 190

Mills Memorial Rose Garden (Syracuse, NY), 180

Mohonk Mountain House Gardens (New Paltz, NY), 178

Montgomery Place (Annandale-on-Hudson, NY), 124

Morris Arboretum (Philadelphia, PA), 199

Mount Vernon Hotel Museum and Garden (New York, NY), 117

Nassau County Museum of Art Sculpture Gardens (Roslyn Harbor, NY), 161

Nemours Mansion and Gardens (Wilmington, DE), 35

New York Botanical Garden (Bronx, NY), 98

New York Chinese Scholar's Garden. *See* Snug Harbor Cultural Center

Noguchi Museum and Sculpture Garden, The (Long Island City, NY), 112

Old Westbury Gardens (Old Westbury, NY), 158

Petrified Sea Gardens (Saratoga Springs, NY), 172

Phipps Conservatory (Pittsburgh, PA), 213

Pittsburgh Civic Garden Center (Pittsburgh, PA), 214

Planting Fields Arboretum (Oyster Bay, NY), 167

Prospect Garden (Princeton, NJ), 88

Queens Botanical Garden (Queens, NY), 119

Ringwood Manor (Ringwood, NJ), 74

Rockwood Gardens (Wilmington, DE), 36

Root Glen (Clinton, NY), 176

Rutgers Gardens (New Brunswick, NJ), 72

𝒮

Salisbury State University Arboretum (Salisbury, MD), 58

Sayen Gardens (Hamilton Township, NJ), 64

Sherwood Gardens (Baltimore, MD), 56

Skylands Botanical Garden (Ringwood, NJ), 77

Snug Harbor Cultural Center (Staten Island, NY), 120

Sonnenberg Gardens (Canandaigua, NY), 175

Springside Restoration (Poughkeepsie, NY), 153

Stonecrop Gardens (Cold Spring, NY), 127

Storm King Art Center (Mountainville, NY), 152

T

Tyler Arboretum (Media, PA), 211

U

Untermyer Park (Yonkers, NY), 154

V

Vanderbilt Mansion Gardens (Hyde Park, NY), 134

W

Waterford Gardens (Saddle River, NJ), 89

Wave Hill (Bronx, NY), 101

West Side Community Garden (New York, NY), 118

Wethersfield Garden (Amenia, NY), 121

William Paca Garden (Annapolis, MD), 45

Willowwood Arboretum (Gladstone, NJ), 85

Winterthur (Winterthur, DE), 38

Wyck (Philadelphia, PA), 212